A Book Of

BUSINESS STATISTICS

For B. Com. – II : Semester – IV
As Per Solapur University's Revised Syllabus
Effective from June 2014

Prof. P. G. DIXIT
M.Sc., M.Phil. (Stats.)
Head of Statistics Department,
Modern College, Pune - 5.

N0484

(B.Com. II) Sem. – IV : BUSINESS STATISTICS   ISBN 978-93-5164-448-4
First Edition   :   January 2015
©   :   Authors

The text of this publication, or any part thereof, should not be reproduced or transmitted in any form or stored in any computer storage system or device for distribution including photocopy, recording, taping or information retrieval system or reproduced on any disc, tape, perforated media or other information storage device etc., without the written permission of Authors with whom the rights are reserved. Breach of this condition is liable for legal action.

Every effort has been made to avoid errors or omissions in this publication. In spite of this, errors may have crept in. Any mistake, error or discrepancy so noted and shall be brought to our notice shall be taken care of in the next edition. It is notified that neither the publisher nor the authors or seller shall be responsible for any damage or loss of action to any one, of any kind, in any manner, therefrom.

Published By :
NIRALI PRAKASHAN
Abhyudaya Pragati, 1312, Shivaji Nagar,
Off J.M. Road, PUNE – 411005
Tel - (020) 25512336/37/39, Fax - (020) 25511379
Email : niralipune@pragationline.com

Printed By :
Repro Knowledgecast Limited
Thane

DISTRIBUTION CENTRES
PUNE

Nirali Prakashan
119, Budhwar Peth, Jogeshwari Mandir Lane
Pune 411002, Maharashtra
Tel : (020) 2445 2044, 66022708, Fax : (020) 2445 1538
Email : bookorder@pragationline.com

Nirali Prakashan
S. No. 28/27, Dhyari,
Near Pari Company, Pune 411041
Tel : (022) 24690371
Email : dhyari@pragationline.com
         bookorder@pragationline.com

MUMBAI
Nirali Prakashan
385, S.V.P. Road, Rasdhara Co-op. Hsg. Society Ltd.,
Girgaum, Mumbai 400004, Maharashtra
Tel : (022) 2385 6339 / 2386 9976, Fax : (022) 2386 9976
Email : niralimumbai@pragationline.com

DISTRIBUTION BRANCHES

NAGPUR
Pratibha Book Distributors
Above Maratha Mandir, Shop No. 3, First Floor,
Rani Jhanshi Square, Sitabuldi, Nagpur 440012,
Maharashtra, Tel : (0712) 254 7129

JALGAON
Nirali Prakashan
34, V. V. Golani Market, Navi Peth, Jalgaon 425001,
Maharashtra, Tel : (0257) 222 0395
Mob : 94234 91860

BENGALURU
Pragati Book House
House No. 1, Sanjeevappa Lane, Avenue Road Cross,
Opp. Rice Church, Bengaluru – 560002.
Tel : (080) 64513344, 64513355,
Mob : 9880582331, 9845021552
Email:bharatsavla@yahoo.com

KOLHAPUR
Nirali Prakashan
New Mahadvar Road,
Kedar Plaza, 1st Floor Opp. IDBI Bank
Kolhapur 416 012, Maharashtra. Mob : 9850046155

CHENNAI
Pragati Books
9/1, Montieth Road, Behind Taas Mahal, Egmore,
Chennai 600008 Tamil Nadu, Tel : (044) 6518 3535,
Mob : 94440 01782 / 98450 21552 / 98805 82331, Email : bharatsavla@yahoo.com

RETAIL OUTLETS
PUNE

Pragati Book Centre
157, Budhwar Peth, Opp. Ratan Talkies,
Pune 411002, Maharashtra
Tel : (020) 2445 8887 / 6602 2707, Fax : (020) 2445 8887

Pragati Book Centre
676/B, Budhwar Peth, Opp. Jogeshwari Mandir,
Pune 411002, Maharashtra
Tel : (020) 6601 7784 / 6602 0855

Pragati Book Centre
Amber Chamber, 28/A, Budhwar Peth,
Appa Balwant Chowk, Pune : 411002, Maharashtra,
Tel : (020) 20240335 / 66281669
Email : pbcpune@pragationline.com

PBC Book Sellers & Stationers
152, Budhwar Peth, Pune 411002, Maharashtra
Tel : (020) 2445 2254 / 6609 2463

MUMBAI
Pragati Book Corner
Indira Niwas, 111 - A, Bhavani Shankar Road, Dadar (W), Mumbai 400028, Maharashtra
Tel : (022) 2422 3526 / 6662 5254, Email : pbcmumbai@pragationline.com

www.pragationline.com   info@pragationline.com

> **Statistical Thinking will one day be necessary for effective citizenship as the ability to read and write**
>
> — H.G. Wells

The book is dedicated to my guru
Prof. D. G. Kulkarni
(Retired Professor of Mathematics at Dayanand College, Solapur)
Who inspired me to learn statistics and gave insight into the subject.
He is my first Statistics Professor at Pre-Degree Science in 1973-74

P. G. Dixit

Preface ...

I am very happy to place this book is in the hands of B.Com. – II : Semester - IV students and professors of Solapur University. The overwhelming response for last 24 years due to the readers has encoureged us every time. This book is written according to new syllabus which comes in force from the academic year 2014. Author has published 76 text books for various classes, considering the background of students and scope of syllabi.

This book will also partly serve the purpose of students preparing for preliminary and intermediate examinations of C.A. and I.C.W.A. While writing the book I have borne in mind that majority of the students have not offered mathematics at XI and XII commerce, so that they are studying mathematics after a break of three years.

Simplicity is a strength of the book, so readers will be interested in studying.

In the present edition, we have simplified the numerical problems and further classified them subtopicwise. It will help all sorts of students from beginers to expert.

We are extremely thankful to our publisher Shri. D. K. Furia, Shri. Jignesh Furia, and staff of Nirali Prakashan especially Mr. Santosh Bare, Mrs. Anagha Medhekar, Mrs. Anjali Mulye for bringing out this book.

The timely help by Prof. Bidwe S. B., Prof. Mumbareddy is well appreciated. The discussion with Dr. S. M. Aherkar made my task simple. Prof. R. V. Rajmane, Prof. N. K. Hipperkar encouraged me. Mr. Prabhakar Nadkile gave me the feedback time-to-time. I sincerely thank all of them.

Suggestions for further improvement of the book will be appreciated and thankfully acknowledged. I whish with this book students will perform well.

Authors

Syllabus ...

1. STATISTICAL QUALITY CONTROL (SCQ) (14)

Concept and need of SQC, Advantages of SQC, Chance and Assignable causes, Process control and Product control.

(i) Control chart for mean and range.

(ii) Control chart for number of defective (np-chart) for a fixed sample size.

(iii) Control chart for number of defects per unit (C-chart).

Numerical examples.

2. INDEX NUMBERS (15)

Need and Meaning of index numbers, Price, Quantity and Value based index numbers, Simple (un-weighted) index numbers Weighted index numbers, Laspeyre's, Paasche's and Fisher's price and quantity index numbers. Simple examples.

3. PROBABILITY AND PROBABILITY DISTRIBUTIONS (16)

Probability : Sample space, Event, Classical definition of probability, Addition and Multiplication laws of probability (without proof). Examples without use of permutation and combination.

Binomial Distribution : Probability mass function (p.m.f.), Mean and Variance (without proof), Simple examples to find probabilities and parameters of the distribution.

Normal Distribution : Probability density function (p.d.f.), Mean and Variance (without proof), Definition of standard normal variate and its p.d.f., Properties of normal curve, Examples to find probabilities for given area under standard normal curve.

4. TIME SERIES (15)

Definition, Components of time series, Methods for determination of trend :

(i) Method of moving averages.

(ii) Method of least squares (only for straight line).

(iii) Method of progressive averages.

Determination of seasonal variation by simple average method. Numerical examples.

Contents ...

1. **Statistical Quality Control**   1.1 – 1.30

2. **Index Number**   2.1 – 2.22

3. **Probability**   3.1 – 3.18

4. **Binomial Probability**   4.1 – 4.10

5. **Normal Distribution**   5.1 – 5.13

6. **Time Series**   6.1 – 6.40

- **Specimen Question Paper**   S.1 – S.3

Chapter 1...
Statistical Quality Control (SQC)

Contents ...
1.1 Introduction
1.2 Quality, SQC and ISO
1.3 Causes of Variation
1.4 Process Control and Lot Control
1.5 Meaning of Statistical Quality Control (S.Q.C.)
1.6 Control Chart and its Construction
1.7 Working of Control Chart
1.8 Basis of Control Limits : 3σ Control Limits
1.9 Criteria for Detecting Lack of Control
1.10 Types of Control Charts
1.11 Control Charts for Variables ($\bar{X}$ and R Charts)
1.12 P-chart and np-chart for Fraction Defective
1.13 C-chart for Number of Defects

Key Words :
SQC, quality, chance cause, assignable cause process control, lot control, control charts, 3σ control limits, $\bar{X}$, R, P, np C charts.

Objectives :
One of the important and elegant application of statistics in manufacturing industry is a control chart. In this chapter one of the on line statistical control technique known as control chart is discussed. ISO 9000, total quality management (TQM) require these techniques.

1.1 Introduction

In modern age due to competition manufacturing companies have to remain very much alert in setting and maintaining quality standards of their products. This task is handled by using various tools of process control. In all there are seven process control tools of which check sheets (tabulation and frequency distribution) scatter diagram and histogram have been introduced to students. The tool control charts is introduced in this chapter. These tools help to ensure the quality and reduce wastages, rework etc. These tools are used right from arrival of raw material to end product. However on line testing is the main work done by SQC in manufacturing processes.

1.2 Quality, SQC and ISO

The word quality will be frequently used in this chapter. Here term quality does not mean the topmost standard but most desirable standard. Many times quality of product can be verified with the help of some dimension such as length, diameter, surface finish, strength. If the specific dimension of item is within the prescribed limits, one can say that it possesses quality. Thus, quality of product means satisfying the requirements of customer. Whenever the variation in the dimension of a product under consideration exceeds the specified limits, we say that the product of quality is poor or inferior.

Quality : The term quality is defined as fitness for use :

One may be interested to know why quality of product changes and how to detect the downfall in quality ? We experience in almost all production situations, variation in the dimension of product is unavoidable. For example, a machine is set with a view to produce the screws of length 3 cm. In the lots produced in the manufacturing process, we observe that length of each screw is not exactly 3 cm. It varies from screw to screw. Every one accepts that small variation is going to be there and accordingly limits for the length may be specified. For example 3.00 ± 0.01 cm. If length of screw does not lie in (3.00 ± 0.01), it will be rejected. The screws non-conforming the specified limits may be considered defective.

At the time of production, manufacturer makes every attempt to maintain the quality. He uses several tools and techniques. Statistical tools such as control charts and sampling plans are used to control the quality of product. These techniques are called as **statistical quality control (SQC) techniques**.

Thus variation is the only cause due to which quality is not maintained. **Quality is inversely proportional to variation**. SQC techniques cannot find causes, however they enable us to detect the entry and presence of such causes. The types of causes, the procedure of detection etc. will be discussed in detail latter.

Use of SQC is not new. Most of the techniques were developed during World War II. Indian standards (IS) and International Standards Organisation (ISO) made use of SQC indispensable in the manufacturing process. ISO increased importance of SQC because it does a third party quality audit. It expects the use of statistical methods in its various clauses and documentation of the results.

1.3 Causes of Variation

Since variation in quality of manufactured product cannot be avoided, one has to search for the causes of variation. These causes are broadly classified in the following two types.

(i) Chance causes (ii) Assignable causes.

(i) Chance Causes :

The causes of variation which are natural and cannot be detected or predicted are called **chance causes.** It is not possible to remove or prevent them. These causes are present in every manufacturing process. The chance cause may be the fluctuations in voltage of electricity. The variation due to these causes is small or negligible. It does not result in producing defective articles to large extent. Variation owing to these causes is called **'chance causes variation'** or **'allowable variation'**.

Chance variations behave in random manner. They obey laws of specific probability distributions. It forms the basis and enables us to develop various techniques to be used in SQC.

(ii) Assignable Causes :

The another category of causes of variation is assignable causes of variation. Many a times such causes can be detected and removed from the production process. For instance poor quality of raw material, different shifts of production, unskilled workers, wrong setting of machine etc. Variation in quality of the product due to these causes is considerable. When such causes enter into a production process, the variation in quality increases to large extent. Consequently the process produces excessive percentage of detective items. Sometimes these causes behave in a non-random or in a systematic way. So they can be identified using statistical techniques. The variation due to these causes is called **assignable causes of variation**. It is also called as **'preventive variation'** as it can be prevented by eliminating these causes. Techniques for identification of assignable causes can be developed.

1.4 Process Control and Lot Control

We apply SQC techniques, mainly in the following two situations.
(i) Process control (on line control)
(ii) Product control or lot control (or off line control)

(i) Process Control :

A manufacturer is interested in maintaining the production process in such a way that percentage of defective articles will be very small and quality of product is reasonably good. This occurs when only chance causes are present in the process. Hence producer wants to ensure that the process is free from any assignable cause of variation. In other words, he desires to achieve on line control. A manufacturing process is said to be under statistical control if the variation in quality of the product is purely due to chance causes. In this situation, the problem is how to identify occurrence of assignable causes ? In other words how to ensure that process is under statistical control ? These questions can be answered by a statistical technique called *'control chart'*. It will be discussed in detail later on.

(ii) Product Control or Lot Control :

Sometimes finished goods, semi-finished goods, raw material or spare parts are purchased by various agencies. It may not be possible to have a lot with all good items. The agencies want to ensure the quality of product in the submitted lots. It is called product control or lot control. Due to several reasons, 100 % inspection of lot is not practicable. SQC technique used in this situation to take decision about accepting or rejecting the lot is known as **'acceptance sampling plans'**.

1.5 Meaning of Statistical Quality Control (S.Q.C.)

S.Q.C. means all statistical methods or procedures which help in evaluating quality standards and improving them. We shall restrict ourselves to statistical techniques used for resolving the problems of process control. The graphical method for examining whether the process is under control or not is, control chart.

1.6 Control Chart and Its Construction

Dr. W.A. Shewart in 1924 first introduced a graphical device to achieve process control called **'control chart'**. It is used to detect presence of assignable causes in the manufacturing process. It gives an alarm or signal as soon as process goes out of control.

It is impracticable to examine whether the process is working properly, continuously for the entire period. Hence it is observed at regular intervals of periods to get feedback about quality of the product.

An item like spring has several characteristics viz inner diameter, outer diameter, tensile strength, elasticity, effect of heat, length etc. Among these some characteristics may directly affect the working of assembled part. These characteristics are called as **critial to quality (CTQ)**. Control charts are used for such CTQ characteristics. Here we develop control chart for only one characteristic at a time.

A control chart is constructed by using following steps :

(1) We draw samples or subgroups at regular interval of time like hourly, daily etc.

(2) The values of characteristic of interest like length, diameter etc. are recorded for every item in sample. The summary statistic like mean, range, proportion etc. is computed for each sample or subgroup.

(3) Along X-axis we take sample number and on Y-axis the characteristic under consideration such as sample mean, sample range etc. choosing suitable scale.

(4) A control chart consists of three lines on this graph viz. Upper Control Limit (U.C.L.), Central Line (C.L.) and Lower Control Limit (L.C.L.). These control limits are determined using probability distribution of summary statistics.

(5) At the end we plot the points corresponding to the statistic computed for each sample or subgroup. These points are called **sample points**.

1.7 Working of Control Chart

The state of control of the process is decided by observing the sample points. Control chart works as follows :

If all sample points lie within control limits on both sides of Central Line (C.L.) at random, we conclude that process is under statistical control with respect to the corresponding characteristic. It means that variation in product is by chance only (due to chance causes).

If one or more sample points fall outside control limits i.e. above U.C.L. or below L.C.L., the control chart signals that process may not be under statistical control. Even though all sample points fall within control limits but show some systematic pattern, the process may not be under control. In such cases control chart indicate presence of assignable causes. Thus a control chart makes us possible to detect assignable causes. A remedial action can be taken to bring the process under statistical control.

1.8 Basis of Control : 3σ Control Limits

Dr. Shewhart first suggested these limits which are constructed using probability theory. Suppose k samples each of size n are drawn at regular intervals of time and for each sample statistic T based on its observations is computed e.g. sample mean, sample range, sample proportion of defectives etc. If the process is under control indicating presence of chance causes alone, T (for CTQ as quantitative variable) follows a specific probability distribution with mean μ and var (T) = σ^2. It is fair enough to assume that the statistic T is normally distributed (i.e. the probability curve is symmetric, bell shaped such that

$P(\mu - \sigma < T < \mu + \sigma) = 0.68$,
$P(\mu - 2\sigma < T < \mu + 2\sigma) = 0.95$
$P(\mu - 3\sigma < T < \mu + 3\sigma) = 0.9973$

Hence we expect that almost all (99.73 %) values of T fall within $(\mu - 3\sigma, \mu + 3\sigma)$ even though theoretically range of T is $(-\infty, \infty)$. Even if population is non-normal, by Tchebycheff's inequality we get

$\therefore \quad P(\mu - 3\sigma < T < \mu + 3\sigma) \geq 0.8889$

Thus in case of non-normal distribution the probability is considerably large. Therefore approximate end points of T can be regarded as $\mu - 3\sigma$ and $\mu + 3\sigma$. So the control limits are taken as

Lower Control Limit (L.C.L.) = $\mu - 3$ S.E. (T)
Control Line (C.L.) = μ.
Upper Control Limit (U.C.L.) = $\mu + 3$ S.E. (T)

These control limits are called 3σ limits as the distance between control limits from C.L. is 3σ.

Remark : In this case probability of taking wrong decision that the process is not under control when in fact it is in control is

$1 - P(\mu - 3\sigma < T < \mu + 3\sigma) = 1 - 0.9973 = 0.0027$.

Sketch of a Control Chart :

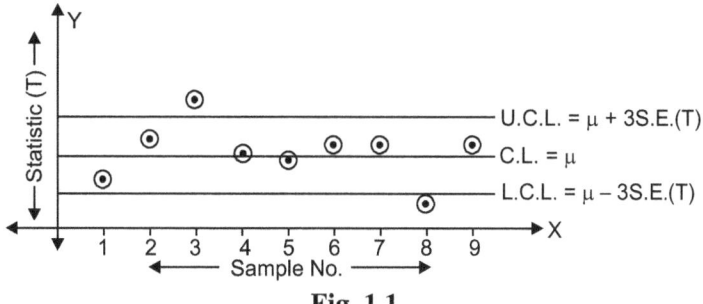

Fig. 1.1

Note : In some cases, the control limits may not be straight lines.

1.9 Criteria for Detecting Lack of Control

The function of control chart is to examine the state of control of the process and give warning when process goes out of control. Therefore it is necessary to study the different criteria to detect lack of control situations. The following are criteria for detecting lack of control.

(i) Obviously, if one or more sample points fall below L.C.L. or above U.C.L. then the control chart indicates that process is out of control. For instance, see the following control chart.

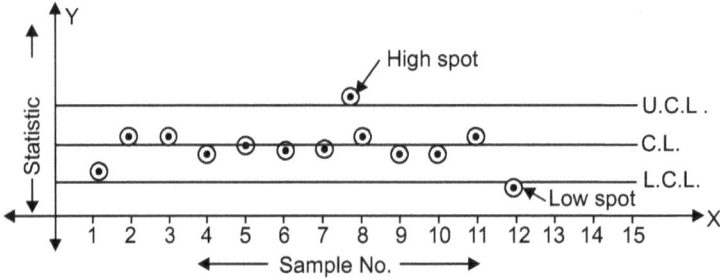

Fig. 1.2 : Chart showing points above UCL or below LCL

In Fig. 1.2 the points corresponding to sample numbers 8 and 12 are above U.C.L. Hence, the control chart indicates lack of control.

(ii) If in a control chart, all sample points lie within control limits but they show presence of cycles, increasing or decreasing trends or any other systematic pattern then it shows that process is not under control. In this case the points give evidence against randomness of chance causes of variation. Some such charts may appear as follows.

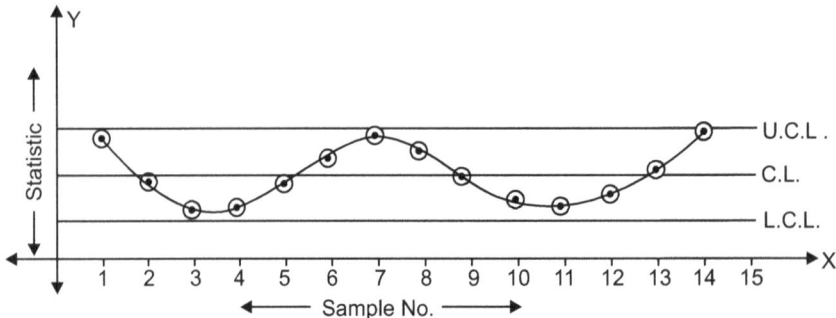

Fig. 1.3 : Chart showing presence of cycles

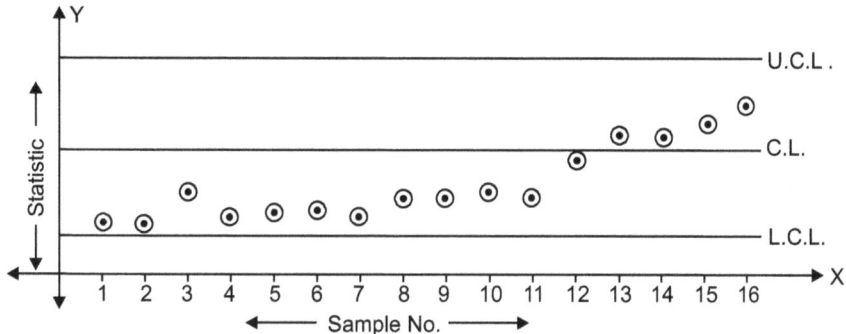

Fig. 1.4 : Chart in which sample points have increasing trend

(iii) If there is a run of 7 or 8 points above central line or below central line in a control chart then it reveals that process is governed by assignable causes. When the process is in control, the chance of observing run of 7 points above (or below) central line is $\left(\frac{1}{2}\right)^7 = \frac{1}{128}$.

Thus, occurrence of such an event is rare if the process is in control.

(iv) The control chart with all sample points too close to central line also supports evidence against random behaviour of chance causes. Hence, it is also one of criterion for detecting lack of control.

1.10 Types of Control Charts

The quantitative characteristics like length, height, thickness, diameter, weight, time etc. are recorded by taking measurements. These characteristics are called **variables**. The control charts used for such characteristics are called **control charts for variables**. In some cases we classify the articles as defective or non-defective. Here characteristic is of **'attribute'** type and the corresponding control charts are called **control charts for attributes**.

1.11 Control Charts for Variables ($\overline{X}$ and R Charts)

When Standards are Given

Many quality characteristics like diameter of a shaft, length of axle of wheel, weight of pauch of oil etc. are continuous variables. These are assumed to be normally distributed with some mean μ and variance σ^2. These parameters completely specify the normal distribution. Hence, process average (μ) and process standard deviation (σ) are called **standards of the process**. When process goes out of control, there is a shift in values of μ or σ or both. However the probability distribution of characteristic remains same.

Although there is a single characteristic under study its probability distribution depends on two parameters μ and σ. Hence, we need to draw two separate control charts. First of all the process variation should be taken care of. Hence, first we construct control chart to examine whether the process is under control with respect to variation within sample. This chart is based on Sample Ranges (R). It is called R-chart. After ensuring that R chart shows state of control of the process, we set-up control chart for process average. It is called $\bar{X}$-chart.

Control charts when the standards are not given :

The standards are unknown means, μ and σ unknown. We have taken n samples each of size n. We find mean $\bar{X}$ for every sample and to measure the variation, we find range.

$$\text{The range} = \begin{bmatrix} \text{The largest observation} \\ \text{in sample} \end{bmatrix} - \begin{bmatrix} \text{The smallest observation} \\ \text{in the sample} \end{bmatrix}$$

Sample No.	1	2	3	4	....	k
Sample mean $\bar{X}$	$\bar{X}_1$	$\bar{X}_2$	$\bar{X}_3$	$\bar{X}_4$	....	$\bar{X}_k$
Sample range R	R_1	R_2	R_3	R_4	....	R_k

R chart consists of the following three lines :

Central line (C.L.) = $\bar{R}$

Upper control limit (U.C.L.) = $D_4 \bar{R}$

Lower control limit (L.C.L.) = $D_3 \bar{R}$.

$\bar{R} = \dfrac{R_1 + R_2 + \ldots + R_k}{k}$ = mean of sample ranges.

D_3 and D_4 are the statistical constants which depend upon the sample size n. The values of D_3 and D_4 are available in statistical tables.

If R chart shows all the points within U.C.L. and L.C.L. without any specific pattern we conclude that the process variation is in control. Then we proceed to check process average.

The process average is checked using $\bar{X}$ chart. It is given by

$$\text{C.L.} = \bar{\bar{X}} = \dfrac{\bar{X}_1 + \bar{X}_2 + \ldots + \bar{X}_k}{K} = \text{mean of sample means}$$

$$\text{U.C.L.} = \bar{\bar{X}} + A_2 \bar{R}$$

$$\text{L.C.L.} = \bar{\bar{X}} - A_2 \bar{R}$$

The values of $\bar{\bar{X}}$ and $\bar{R}$ are to be computed using the sample values. A_2 is a statistical constant available in table for various values of n.

The estimate of process average is $\bar{\bar{X}}$. The estimate of process standard deviation is $\dfrac{\bar{R}}{d_2}$, where, d_2 is a statistical constant available in statistical table for various values of n.

Solved Examples

Example 1.1 : Fourteen samples of 4 electric bulbs each are drawn at intervals of one hour from a production process. The following data give average life and the range for 14 samples.

Sample No.	1	2	3	4	5	6	7
Mean ($\bar{X}$)	930	1010	980	950	1020	990	1050
Range (R)	150	180	90	120	210	120	135
Sample No.	8	9	10	11	12	13	14
Mean ($\bar{X}$)	940	980	990	990	1005	970	1010
Range (R)	150	240	105	165	180	75	60

Construct the appropriate control charts and write conclusion [Given that for n = 4, the constants are $d_2 = 2.059$, $D_3 = 0$, $D_4 = 2.282$, $A_2 = 0.729$.

Also estimate process average and process standard deviation.

Solution : R chart : $\bar{R} = \dfrac{\sum R}{k} = \dfrac{1980}{14} = 141.43$ k = number of samples = 14

$$\text{U.C.L.} = D_4 \bar{R} = 2.282 \times 141.43 = 322.74$$

$$\text{L.C.L.} = D_3 \bar{R} = 0 \times 141.43 = 0$$

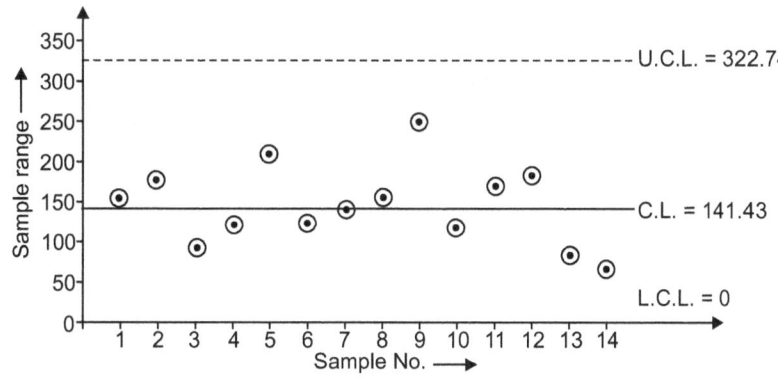

Fig. 1.5

Interpretation : Since all the points on R chart lie within control limits and those are scattered in random manner the process variation is in statistical control.

We proceed further for $\bar{X}$ chart.

$$\text{C.L.} = \bar{\bar{X}} = \dfrac{\sum \bar{X}}{k} = \dfrac{13815}{14} = 986.79$$

$$\text{U.C.L.} = \bar{\bar{X}} + A_2\bar{R} = 986.79 + 0.729 \times 141.40 = 1089.87$$

$$\text{L.C.L.} = \bar{\bar{X}} - A_2\bar{R} = 986.79 - 0.729 \times 141.40 = 883.71$$

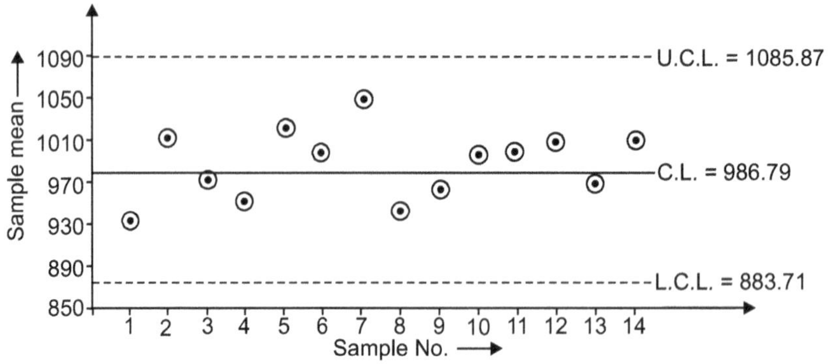

Fig. 1.6

From the above chart we see that all the points on $\bar{X}$ chart are within control limits, moreover the points are scattered in random manner. We conclude that the process average is in statistical control.

Thus, both the characteristics viz. process variation and process average are in statistical control. Estimate of process average is $\bar{\bar{X}} = 986.79$. Estimate of process variation is $\dfrac{\bar{R}}{d_2} = \dfrac{141.43}{2.059} = 68.69$.

Example 1.2 : Thirteen samples of size 6 each are drawn from the production process after every three hours. The values of means and ranges for each of the thirteen samples were as follows :

Sample No.	1	2	3	4	5	6	7
Mean ($\bar{X}$)	190	225	200	220	250	285	260
Range (R)	45	85	75	40	90	110	80
Sample No.	8	9	10	11	12	13	
Mean ($\bar{X}$)	240	230	275	180	195	240	
Range (R)	65	55	170	85	50	70	

Draw appropriate control chart to examine that the process is under control [Given that for n = 6, $D_3 = 0$, $d_2 = 2.534$, $D_4 = 2.004$, $A_2 = 0.483$.

Suggest the control limits for future.

Solution : First of all we draw R chart.

Here, n = Size of each sample = 6, k = Number of samples = 13

$$\text{C.L.} = \bar{R} = \frac{\Sigma R}{k} = \frac{1020}{13} = 78.46$$

$$\text{U.C.L.} = D_4 \bar{R} = 2.004 \times 78.46 = 151.24$$

$$\text{L.C.L.} = D_3 \bar{R} = 0 \times 78.46 = 0$$

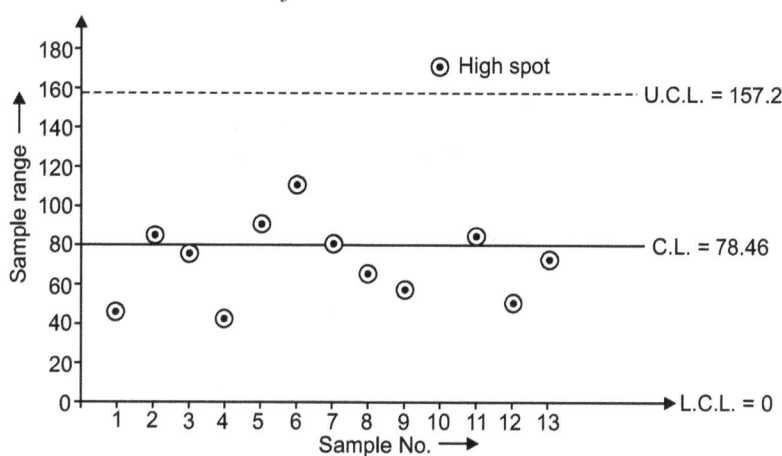

Fig. 1.7

Interpretation : Sample number 10 on R chart goes beyond U.C.L., hence it is indication of lack of control. Hence, process is out of statistical control with respect to process variation. We do not proceed for $\bar{X}$ chart.

Remark : Further the point showing lack of control is omitted and control limits are recalculated till all the points lie within control limits. Such limits are used in future. With those limits $\bar{X}$ chart is plotted. $\bar{X}$ chart is plotted for those observations for which R chart is in control. $\bar{X}$ chart is revised if needed. However, once R chart is finalised it need not be revised.

In the above problem, after eliminating sample point 10, we get

$$\bar{R} = \frac{850}{12} = 70.83$$

$$\text{U.C.L.} = D_4 \bar{R} = 2.004 \times 70.83 = 141.95$$

$$\text{L.C.L.} = D_3 \bar{R} = 0 \times 70.83 = 0$$

With these limits we see that all the points lie within control. We draw $\bar{X}$ chart with the remaining 12 sample points.

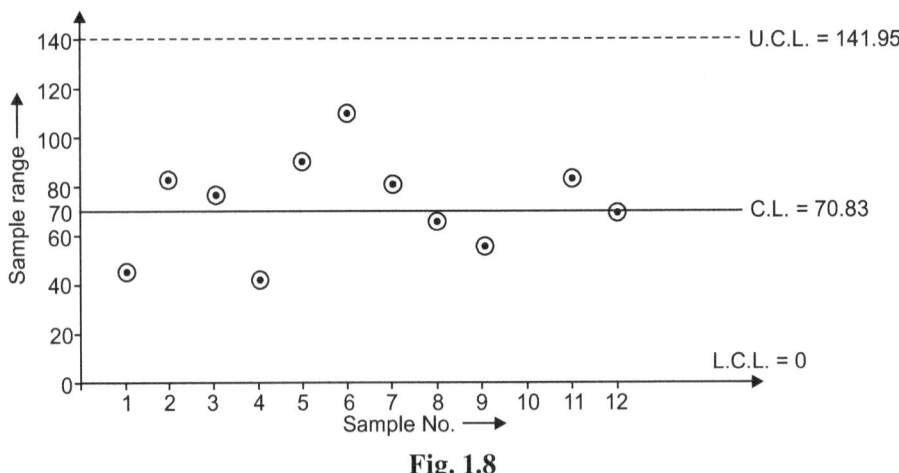

Fig. 1.8

To find $\bar{X}$ chart (excluding sample point number 10)

$$\text{C.L.} = \bar{\bar{X}} = \frac{\sum \bar{X}}{12} = \frac{2715}{12} = 226.25$$

$$\text{U.C.L.} = \bar{\bar{X}} + A_2 \bar{R} = 226.25 + (0.483 \times 70.83)$$
$$= 260.46$$

$$\text{L.C.L.} = \bar{\bar{X}} - A_2 \bar{R} = 226.25 - (0.483 \times 70.83)$$
$$= 192.04$$

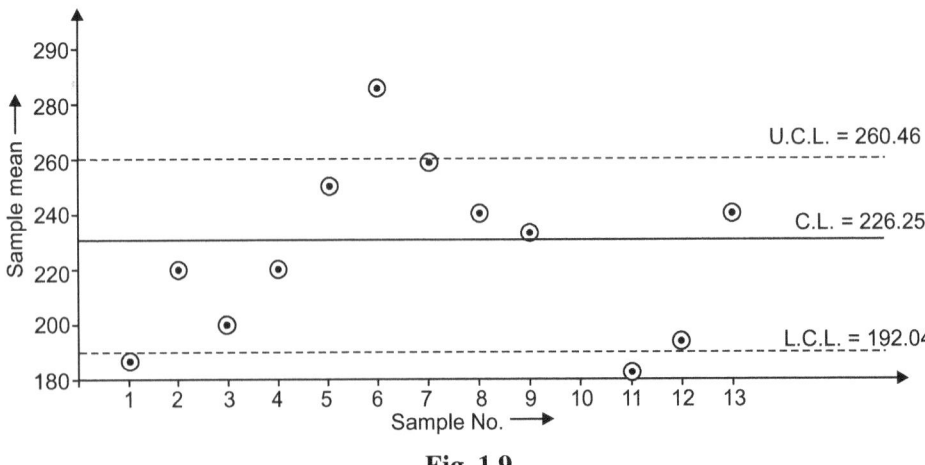

Fig. 1.9

From the above $\bar{X}$ chart, we see that sample point no. 6 is above U.C.L. (High spot). The sample point no. 1 and 11 are below. L.C.L. (low spots), hence the process average is out of control.

To find the limits for further use, we delete those points and recompute $\bar{\bar{X}}$ with remaining 9 observations.

$$\bar{\bar{X}} = \frac{2060}{9} = 228.89$$

With the new value of $\bar{\bar{X}}$ we compute U.C.L. and L.C.L.

$$\text{U.C.L.} = \bar{\bar{X}} - A_2\bar{R} = 228.89 + (0.483 \times 70.83)$$
$$= 263.10$$

$$\text{L.C.L.} = \bar{\bar{X}} + A_2\bar{R} = 228.89 - (0.483 \times 70.83)$$
$$= 194.68$$

For these U.C.L., L.C.L. process average is in control. Hence,

Estimate of process average for future $= \bar{\bar{X}} = 228.89$.

Estimate of process standard deviation $= \dfrac{\bar{R}}{d_2} = \dfrac{70.83}{2.534} = 27.95$.

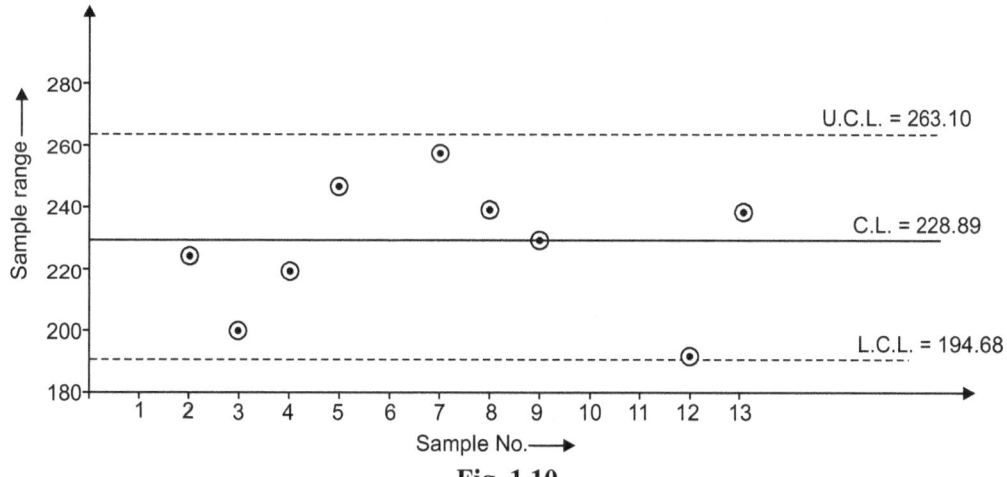

Fig. 1.10

Example 1.3 : Following are 10 samples each of size 5 giving the diameter of cap of bottle measured in suitable units.

Sample No.	1	2	3	4	5	6	7	8	9	10
Diameter	33	28	40	28	20	23	32	36	22	22
	27	27	22	25	32	37	22	25	22	20
	22	22	37	22	30	22	18	22	23	30
	21	25	23	26	20	20	20	22	28	30
	27	18	28	23	18	23	23	25	25	23

Is the process under statistical control ?

Given that for n = 5, $D_3 = 0$, $D_4 = 2.115$, $A_2 = 0.577$.

Solution : For the above data we compute sample mean ($\bar{X}$) and sample range (R) for each sample.

Sample No.	Total of observations $\sum X$	Sample Mean $\bar{X}$	Largest observation L	Smallest observation S	Range R = L – S
1	130	26	33	21	12
2	120	24	28	18	10
3	150	30	40	22	18
4	124	24.8	28	22	6
5	120	24	32	18	14
6	125	25	37	20	17
7	115	23	32	18	14
8	130	26	36	22	14
9	120	24	28	22	6
10	125	25	30	20	10
Total	–	251.8	–	–	121

To check whether process variation is in control, we use R chart.

$$\text{C.L.} = \bar{R} = \frac{121}{10} = 12.1$$

$$\text{U.C.L.} = D_4 \bar{R} = 2.115 \times 12.1 = 25.59$$

$$\text{L.C.L.} = D_3 \bar{R} = 0 \times 12.1 = 0$$

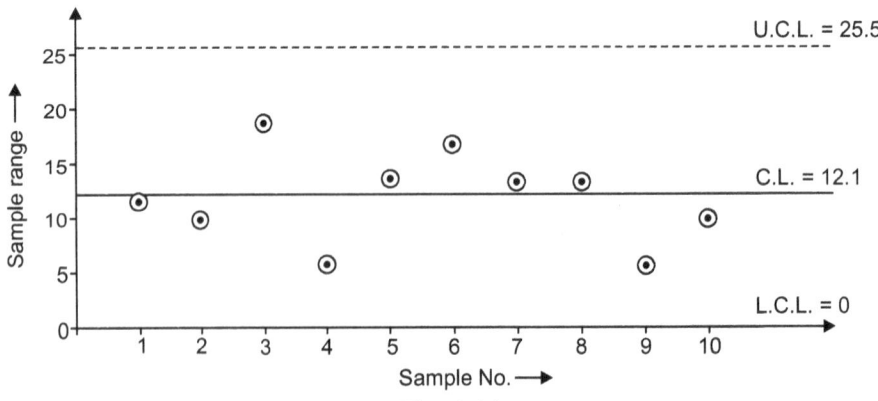

Fig. 1.11

From the above figure we conclude that process variation is under statistical control.

To check whether process average is in control we use $\bar{X}$ chart

$$\text{C.L.} = \frac{\sum \bar{X}}{k} = \bar{\bar{X}} = \frac{251.8}{10} = 25.18$$

$$\text{U.C.L.} = \bar{\bar{X}} + A_2 \bar{R} = 25.18 + (0.577 \times 12.1) = 32.16$$
$$\text{L.C.L.} = \bar{\bar{X}} - A_2 \bar{R} = 25.18 - (0.577 \times 12.1) = 18.20$$

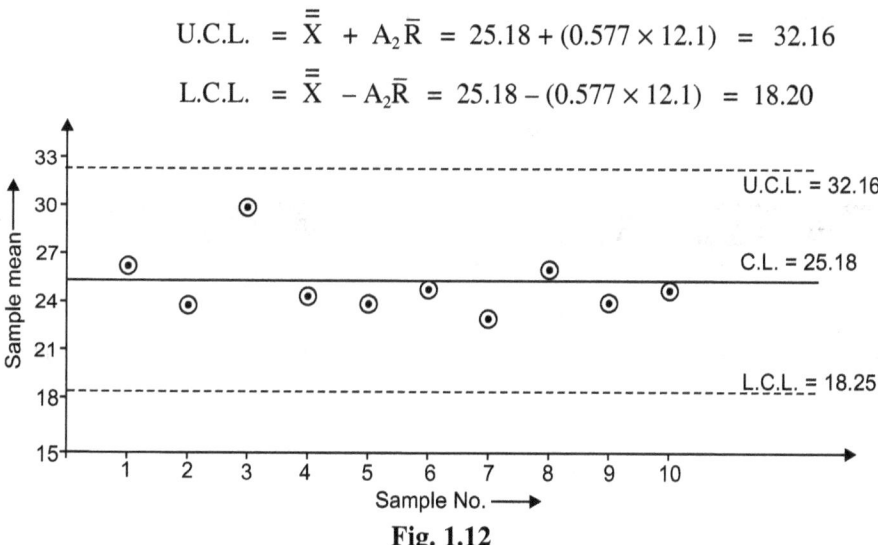

Fig. 1.12

The above figure shows that the process is under statistical control.

Limitations of $\bar{X}$ and R Chart :

(1) If the observations are qualitative in nature, $\bar{X}$ and R charts are not applicable. For example, the items are classified as defective or non-defective, in this situation we do not record any characteristic. We count number of defective items.

Sometimes number of defects or imperfections per item are counted and no record is available by the method of measurement.

(2) Sometimes two or more variable characteristics are measured and checked, in that situation univariate charts are not proper. Multivariate control charts are not simple to use. For example, suppose item has three important characteristics such as length, breadth and thickness. One has to use three $\bar{X}$, R charts one for each characteristic or use multivariate control chart.

To overcome the limitation (1) P and C charts are developed.

Types of Measurement :

As far as SQC is concerned, we use two types of measurements. viz. variable and attributes.

Variable : Quantitative characteristics such as length, breadth, thickness, diameter, pitch, voltage, amount of current, tensile strength are called as **'variables'**. The record of these characteristics is by measurement.

We use $\bar{X}$, R chart for variables.

Attributes : Qualitative characteristic is called as **'attribute'**.

Whether a particular characteristic is according to given norms is verified. If it is within norms or specifications it is taken as good otherwise defective.

For example : If the length of screw is within specifications, it is taken to be good. If the inner diameter of spring is within norms it is considered good. If the tensile strength of spring is within norm the spring is good otherwise it is defective.

The record by classifying the object to be good or defective is a record by attributes. We cannot use $\bar{X}$, R charts for attributes. In this case, we use P chart, C chart.

1.12 P Chart or Control Chart for Fraction Defective

Suppose we take k samples each of size n chosen from the manufactured lot at a regular intervals for quality control activity.

Defective item : An item is said to be defective if it fails to confirm one or more specifications.

All the items from sample are inspected and classified as good or defective. Suppose there are d defectives in a sample of size n.

Then,

$$\begin{pmatrix} \text{Fraction defective} \\ \text{or} \\ \text{proportion of defectives} \end{pmatrix} = \frac{\text{Number of items defective}}{\text{Number of items inspected}}$$

$$p = \frac{d}{n}$$

Theoretical Basis of P Chart :

(1) The variation due to chance causes in p will behave in random manner.
(2) The number of defectives (d) follows binomial distribution.
(3) There will be no runs, cycles, trends, or any systematic pattern of variation due to chance causes.
(4) Almost all values of p will lie between 3 sigma limits if there is no assignable cause of variation.

Construction of P Chart :

Suppose the samples of fixed size n are chosen at regular interval. The process is set for fraction defective target value P. The control limits will be given by

$$\text{C.L.} = \bar{P}$$

$$\text{U.C.L.} = \bar{P} + 3\sqrt{\frac{\bar{P}\bar{Q}}{n}}$$

$$\text{L.C.L.} = \bar{P} - 3\sqrt{\frac{\bar{P}\bar{Q}}{n}}$$

where, $\bar{P} = \frac{\sum P}{k}$ and $\bar{Q} = 1 - \bar{P}$

Note : If L.C.L. < 0 take it zero, because p cannot be negative.

Working of P Chart :

If all the observations lie in L.C.L. and U.C.L. without any specific pattern then we conclude that the process is under statistical control.

Solved Examples

Example 1.4 : Ten samples each of size 200 were taken from a manufacturing process of switches. The number of defectives were found to be as follows :

8, 10, 12, 9, 14, 12, 6, 3, 13, 5

Does the process appear to exhibit statistical control ?

Solution : We find fraction defective for each sample. Here the samples are of size $n = 200$. The number of samples $(k) = 10$.

Sample No.	1	2	3	4	5	6	7	8	9	10
No. of defectives in sample (d)	8	10	12	9	14	12	6	3	13	5
Fraction defective, $p = \dfrac{d}{n}$	0.04	0.05	0.06	0.045	0.07	0.06	0.03	0.015	0.065	0.025

$$\bar{P} = \frac{\Sigma p}{k}$$

$$\bar{P} = \frac{0.04 + 0.05 + \ldots + 0.025}{k}, \quad k = 10$$

$$\bar{P} = \frac{0.46}{10} = 0.046$$

$\therefore \qquad$ C.L. $= \bar{P} = 0.046$

$\therefore \qquad \bar{Q} = 1 - \bar{P} = 1 - 0.046 = 0.954$

$$\text{U.C.L.} = \bar{P} + 3\sqrt{\frac{\bar{P}\bar{Q}}{n}}$$

$$= 0.046 + 3\sqrt{\frac{0.046 \times 0.954}{200}}$$

$$= 0.046 + 3 \times 0.014813$$

$$= 0.0904$$

$$\text{L.C.L.} = \bar{P} - 3\sqrt{\frac{\bar{P}\bar{Q}}{3}}$$

$$= 0.046 - 3\sqrt{\frac{0.046 \times 0.954}{200}}$$

$$= 0.046 - 3 \times 0.014813$$

$$= 0.001560$$

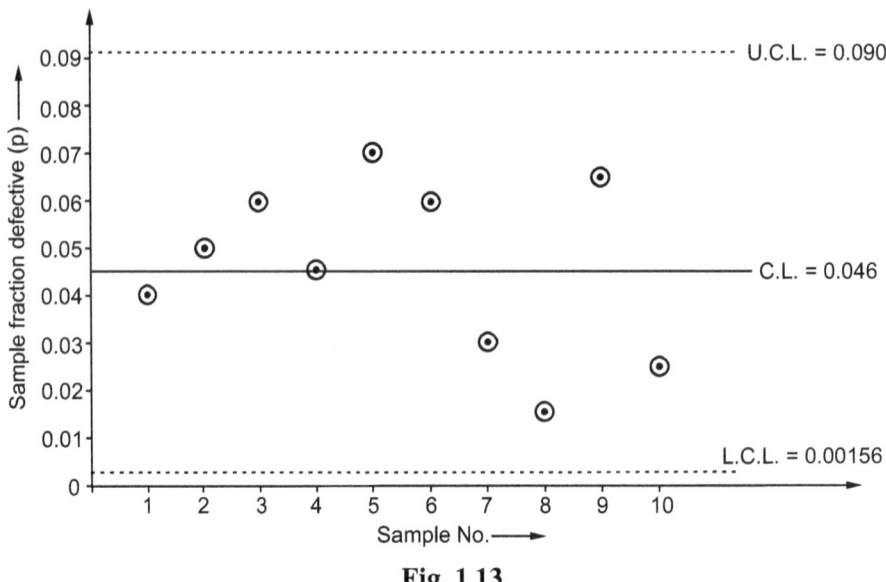

Fig. 1.13

Interpretation : Since all the points lie within L.C.L. and U.C.L., the points are scattered in random manner, the process is under statistical control.

Example 1.5 : The fraction defectives in a lot of 12 samples each of 100 were as follows :

0.01, 0.02, 0.01, 0.03, 0.04, 0.09, 0.06, 0.15, 0.0, 0.01, 0.05, 0.04.

Is the process under statistical control ?

Solution : Here n = 100 = The size of sample

$$k = 12 = \text{The number of samples}$$

$$\text{C.L.} = \bar{P} = \frac{\Sigma P}{k} = \frac{0.51}{12} = 0.0425$$

$$\text{U.C.L.} = \bar{P} + 3\sqrt{\frac{\bar{P}\bar{Q}}{n}}$$

$$= 0.0425 + 3\sqrt{\frac{0.0425 \times 0.9575}{100}}$$

$$= 0.0425 + 0.06052 \qquad (\because \bar{Q} = 1 - \bar{P} = 1 - 0.0425)$$

$$= 0.10302$$

$$\text{L.C.L.} = \bar{P} - 3\sqrt{\frac{\bar{P}\bar{Q}}{n}} = 0.0425 - 3\sqrt{\frac{0.0425 \times 0.9575}{100}}$$

$$= -0.01802$$

Note that P cannot be negative, hence we take L.C.L. = 0.

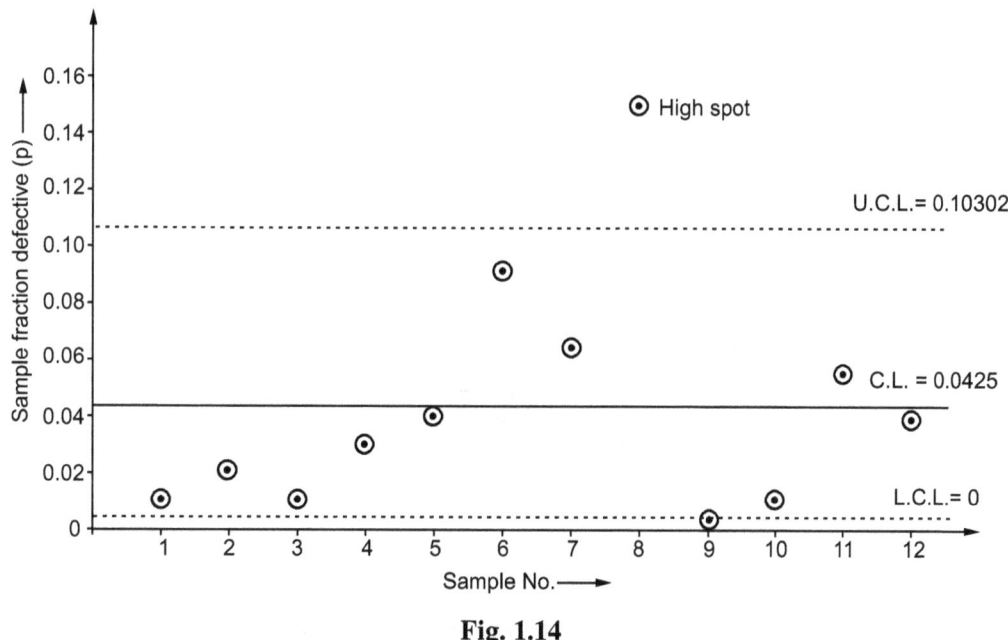

Fig. 1.14

Interpretation : Since sample number 8 goes beyond U.C.L., process is out of statistical control. There may be some assignable cause. It may be identified and removed latter on.

High spot : The point above U.C.L. is called as **high spot**. It indicates the presence of assignable cause, due to which proportion of defective is increased.

Low spot : The point below L.C.L. is called as low spot. It also indicates the presence of assignable cause. The point below L.C.L. is an indication of improvement in quality. Sudden improvement in quality is not a natural phenomenon. So we should look for a cause behind it. The cause may be good or bad. For example, decrease in value of p may due to excellent raw material, sophisticated instruments, uninterrupted power supply. Those are good causes, however those are assignable causes. Measures may be taken to improve the quality. On the other hand decrease in p may be due to mistake in record. Suppose instead of 18 defectives 8 are recorded. It is likely to produce low spot. There may be a untrained supervisor who can not distinguish properly the good or bad items. There may be tendency of passing the bad items. If may reduce the value of p, which ultimately results into low spots.

nP chart or d chart (chart for number of defectives)

Sometimes the value of fraction defective p is very small; in this case P chart is inconvenient. In stead of P chart, nP chart (or d chart is used). In nP chart we use d the number of defectives inspected in a lot of size n. The rest of the procedure is similar to P chart.

Suppose these are k lots each of size n.

Lot No.	1	2	...	k	Total
No. of defectives	d_1	d_3	...	d_k	$\sum d$

The average of $d = \bar{d} = \dfrac{\sum d}{k}$.

$$C.L. = \bar{d}$$

$$LCL = \bar{d} - 3\sqrt{\dfrac{\bar{d}(n - \bar{d})}{n}}$$

$$UCL = \bar{d} + 3\sqrt{\dfrac{\bar{d}(n - \bar{d})}{n}}$$

Illustration 1 : The following are the number of defectives found in 10 lots of size 2000 each, draw nP chart and comment on the statistical control of the process.

2, 5, 3, 2, 2, 1, 4, 5, 3, 3.

Solution : No. of groups (k) = 10, Size of each group (n) = 2000.

Total number of defectives = $\sum d = 28$.

$$\bar{d} = \dfrac{\sum d}{k} = \dfrac{30}{10} = 3, \quad (n - \bar{d}) = 2000 - 3 = 1997$$

$$CL = \bar{d} = 3$$

$$LCL = \bar{d} - 3\sqrt{\dfrac{\bar{d}(n - \bar{d})}{n}}$$

$$= 3 - 3\sqrt{\dfrac{3 \times 1997}{2000}} = 3 - 5.19225 = -2.1925$$

(We take LCL = 0, if it is negative, we take it zero.)

$$UCL = 8.19923$$

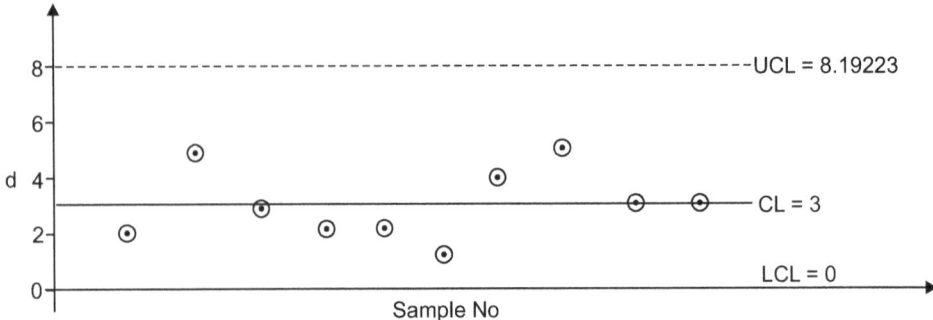

Fig. 1.15

Conclusion : Since all the points are within (LCL, UCL) and they are scattered at random, process is in statistical control.

Limitations of P and nP-Chart :

(1) If sample size n is not fixed the procedure is more complicated.

(2) P chart considers all characteristics together. We do not get idea whether item is defective due to one or many characteristics.

(3) It is advisable to use p chart for fixed number of characteristics.

To overcome limitations (2) we propose C chart.

1.13 C Chart or Control Chart for Number of Defects

Many times items are checked after the assembly. For example, testing of computer after assembly, engine, watch, T.V. set, car music system, insulated wire, refrigerator, washing machine, fabric etc.

In such inspection, the number of defects per item is measured. We denote it by C. The control chart for C is obtained by, counting number of defects for k observations. Clearly C_1, C_2, ..., C_k will be the number of defects. This gives

$$\text{Average number of defects} = \bar{C} = \frac{C_1 + C_2 + \ldots + C_k}{k}$$

The C chart is given by

$$\text{C.L.} = \bar{C}$$

$$\text{U.C.L.} = \bar{C} + 3\sqrt{\bar{C}}$$

$$\text{L.C.L.} = \bar{C} - 3\sqrt{\bar{C}}$$

Note : We know that C cannot be negative, so we take L.C.L. = 0 if it is negative.

Example 1.6 : The following are imperfections observed on each of ten carpets manufactured by a ABC textile company.

8, 9, 5, 8, 5, 9, 9, 11, 4, 12.

Is the process under statistical control ?

Solution : In the above problem we count the number of defectives per item, hence we use C chart. There are (k = 10) observations.

$$\text{C.L.} = \bar{C} = \frac{\Sigma C}{k} = \frac{8 + 9 + 5 + \ldots + 12}{10} = \frac{80}{10} = 8$$

$$\text{U.C.L.} = \bar{C} + 3\sqrt{\bar{C}} = 8 + 3\sqrt{8} = 8 + 8.49 = 16.49$$

$$\text{L.C.L.} = \bar{C} - 3\sqrt{\bar{C}} = 8 - 3\sqrt{8} = 8 - 8.49 = -0.49 < 0$$

∴   L.C.L. = 0

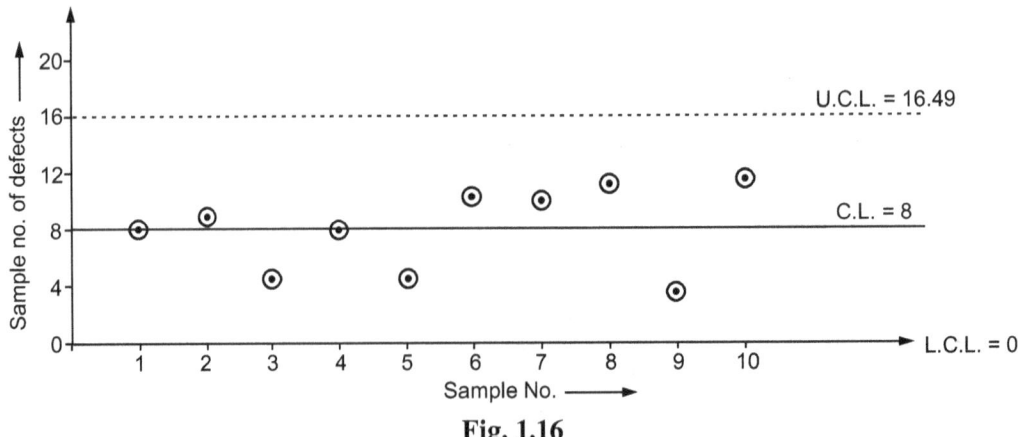

Fig. 1.16

Interpretation : Since all the points are within control limits, and the points are scattered in random manner process is within statistical control.

Exercise 1 (A)

1. Explain the need of statistical quality control.
2. Distinguish between chance causes and assignable causes of variation.
3. Describe in brief the construction of a control chart.
4. What is a control chart ? State the working of a control chart.
5. Explain the terms process control, quality, statistical quality control.
6. (a) Explain the basis of a control chart.
   (b) What are 3σ limits ? Why they are used in control charts ?
7. A production process is known to be in statistical control. Does this indicate that it is free from variation in quality ? Justify your answer.
8. Explain the term 'control charts for variables'.
9. State different criteria for detecting lack of control of the process from a control chart.
10. Describe in brief the construction of $\bar{X}$ and R charts for the measurable quality characteristic when standards are given.
11. Answer the following :
    (a) Why do we plot $\bar{X}$ and R charts and not $\bar{X}$ chart alone ?
    (b) If R chart shows lack of control, would you proceed to plot $\bar{X}$ chart ? Why ?

12. State the objectives of statistical quality control.
13. Define the terms (i) defective item, (ii) defect, (iii) fraction defective, (iv) percent defective.
14. Distinguish between defect and defective.
15. Explain the construction and working of control chart for fraction defectives (p chart) for standards unknown.
16. Explain the construction and working of np chart when standards are unknown.
17. Explain the construction and working of control charts for number of defect per item (c chart); when standards are unknown.
18. Compare the advantages and disadvantages of control charts for variables with those of control charts for attributes.
19. State the situations for C chart.
20. State giving reasons, which control chart is appropriate in the following situations :
    (i) The number of weak spot in an insulated in a given length of insulated wire subjected to a specified voltage.
    (ii) Resistance in ohms of certain electrical component.
    (iii) The number of seeds observed in a glass bottle.
    (iv) The number cracked vessels per case of n vessels.
    (v) Number of defects in computer.

Exercise 1 (B)

1. A machine is set to produce a certain type of discs. 15 samples of size 5 are taken hourly and average thickness (in mm) is measural. Ranges for all samples were recorded as follows :

Sample no.	1	2	3	4	5	6	7	8
Mean	8.8	9.2	8.9	9.3	9.1	8.6	9.0	9.2
Range	0.9	1.2	1.6	1.0	2.0	1.8	1.7	0.8
Sample no.	9	10	11	12	13	14	15	
Mean	9.4	9.1	8.7	8.8	9.3	9.0	9.2	
Range	1.2	1.4	2.0	1.1	1.9	2.1	1.1	

Draw control chart for mean and range and conclude whether the process is under control. [Given for n = 5, $D_3 = 0$, $d_2 = 2.326$, $D_4 = 2.115$, $A_2 = 0.577$]

2. A manufacturing process is expected to pack sacks of sugar. 20 samples of 4 sacks each are drawn after regular interval of time. The mean weight and range (in kg) for these are computed as given below.

Sample no.	1	2	3	4	5	6	7
Mean	49	50.2	49.6	50.1	51	49.6	51.5
Range	1.5	2.1	1.3	2.0	1.6	2.2	2.4
Sample no.	8	9	10	11	12	13	14
Mean	51.4	50	50.5	50.2	49	49.8	50.5
Range	2.7	1.6	1.8	1.7	2.5	2.8	2.6
Sample no.	15	16	17	18	19	20	
Mean	51	50	49.9	49.3	49.6	50.7	
Range	1.4	1.3	2.8	1.4	1.8	2.4	

Using appropriate control charts examine the state of control of the process. [Given for n = 4, $D_3 = 0$, $d_2 = 2.059$, $D_4 = 2.282$, $A_2 = 0.729$].

3. A production process of lighters is to be maintained. From this process 16 samples of size 6 were drawn after 8 hours. The arithmetic means and ranges (in cm) for these samples were recorded as follows :

Sample no.	1	2	3	4	5	6	7	8
Mean	18.1	17.9	18.2	18.5	17.8	18	18.2	18.3
Range	0.4	0.6	0.5	0.7	0.8	0.7	0.9	1.0
Sample no.	9	10	11	12	13	14	15	16
Mean	20	19	18.6	17.9	21	19	18.9	18.8
Range	1.2	0.9	1.0	0.8	1.3	0.6	0.8	0.9

[Given for n = 6, $D_3 = 0$, $d_2 = 2.534$, $D_4 = 2.004$, $A_2 = 0.483$]

Comment on the state of the process using appropriate control charts.

4. Below are given the means and ranges of 12 samples of size 5 each taken from a certain production process at regular intervals.

Sample no.	1	2	3	4	5	6
Mean ($\bar{X}$)	23.2	25.7	24.9	24.3	25.1	22.9
Range (R)	3.1	3.5	2.9	3.7	2.4	3.7
Sample no.	7	8	9	10	11	12
Mean ($\bar{X}$)	26.1	27.9	24.7	22.8	22.6	28.5
Range (R)	2.4	3.6	2.5	4.0	6.0	3.3

Examine whether the process is under statistical control using the appropriate control charts. [It is given that for n = 5, $D_3 = 0$, $d_2 = 2.326$, $D_4 = 2.115$, $A_2 = 0.577$].

5. For 20 samples each of size 4, $\sum \bar{X} = 41.20$ and $\sum R = 0.34$. Compute 3 sigma limits for $\bar{X}$ and R charts. Also estimate the process average and process standard deviation. (For n = 4, $A_2 = 0.729$, $D_3 = 0$, $D_4 = 2.282$.)

6. A pharmaceutical company employs quality control technique to control the concentration of a certain ingredient in their product. Ten samples each of size 3 were taken, which are summerised below.

Sample No.	1	2	3	4	5	6	7	8	9	10
$\bar{X}$	10.2	10.5	10.4	10.3	9.75	10.2	10.2	10.4	10.3	9.75
R	0.45	0.69	0.53	0.15	0.55	0.24	0.11	0.71	0.9	0.55

Can you say that the process is under statistical control ? (For n = 3, A_2 = 1.023, D_3 = 0, D_4 = 2.575.)

7. Following are transaction times (in sec) at a bank at busy hours on 10 working days observed for 5 customers.

Day	Transaction time for 5 customers in (sec.)
1	126, 110, 112, 106, 121
2	120, 126, 120, 130, 122
3	114, 120, 122, 130, 132
4	116, 128, 120, 122, 114
5	158, 136, 130, 121, 148
6	110, 132, 124, 126, 112
7	114, 122, 116, 128, 112
8	116, 102, 122, 114, 132
9	130, 132, 124, 136, 122
10	146, 132, 122, 140, 144

Construct the suitable control chart and comment on the process of transaction.

For n = 5, D_3 = 0, D_4 = 2.115, A_2 = 0.577

8. Following are the data on life of battery in days for a batch of 5 batteries.

Batch No.	$\bar{X}$	R	Batch No.	$\bar{X}$	R
1	1850	50	7	1885	68
2	1785	56	8	1805	58
3	1690	60	9	1790	63
4	1900	45	10	1860	75
5	1830	90	11	1795	82
6	1790	72	12	1670	70

Is process under statistical control ?

For n = 5, D_3 = 0, D_4 = 2.115, A_2 = 0.577

9. An automatic filling machine was observed for 10 samples each of 100 bottles. The number of bottles underfilled were as follows :

Sample No.	1	2	3	4	5	6	7	8	9	10
No. of under-filled bottles	6	7	4	5	12	10	8	7	10	12

Construct a suitable chart and comment on the working of machine.

10. The percent defectives for 12 lots each of size 200 in a production process of tyres are given below :

Lot No.	1	2	3	4	5	6	7	8	9	10	11	12
Percent defectives	2	1.5	0.5	1.5	2	2.5	2	1	3	3.5	0	2

Can you conclude whether the process is in control ?

11. Number of leak milk bags found in a lot of 100 bags were as follows :

Sample No.	1	2	3	4	5	6	7	8	9	10
No. of leak bags	2	0	3	5	4	3	1	2	0	5

Is the sealing process under control ? Use (i) p chart, (ii) np chart.

12. The number of pointess screws considered to be defective were recorded lot of 500 size each as follows :

Sample No.	1	2	3	4	5	6	7	8
No. of defectives	50	48	65	35	62	18	28	10

Is the process under statistical control ?

13. The oversize washers were considered to be defective. Eight lots of size 80 each gave the following record. Use (i) p chart, (ii) np chart.

Lot No.	1	2	3	4	5	6	7	8
No. of defectives	12	8	10	9	5	14	3	8

Is the process under statistical control ?

14. The number of defects found in 10 computers are as follows :

2, 5, 6, 0, 3, 4, 5, 3, 2, 1.

Can you conclude that the assembled computers are under statistically controlled process ?

15. Number of defects per car are given below :

5, 8, 3, 2, 5, 12, 11, 10, 6, 2, 12, 10.

Is the manufacturing process under control ?

16. Following are the imperfections found on insulated wire for 10 pieces each of 5 metre length. 4, 5, 2, 7, 0, 3, 5, 2, 1, 6.

Is the process under statistical control ?

17. The number of imperfections found on a fabric of per 1 metre length for a 10 metre continuous sheet.

5, 3, 8, 4, 2, 1, 0, 5, 2, 6.

Is there any evidence that the process is not under statistical control ?

Answers

	R-chart				$\bar{X}$ chart			
	LCL	CL	UCL	Decision	LCL	CL	UCL	Decision
1.	0	1.4533	3.0738	In control	8.2014	9.04	9.8786	In control
2.	0	1.995	4.5526	In control	48.6906	50.145	51.5994	In control
3.	0	0.81875	1.6408	In control	18.2420	18.6375	19.033	Out of control
4.	0	3.425	7.2439	In control	22.9230	24.8992	26.8754	Out of control
5.	0	0.017	0.03804	In control	2.05019	2.06	2.09879	Out of control
6.	0	0.488	1.2566	In control	5.7001	10.2	10.699	Out of control
7.	0	20.5	43.3575	In control	42.4515	124.28	136.10	Out of control
8.	0	65.75	139.06	In control	1766.2293	1804.107	1842.10	Out of control

	P chart				np chart			
	LCL	CL	UCL	Decision	LCL	CL	UCL	Decision
9	0	0.081	0.16285	In control	–	–	–	–
10.	0	0.01792	0.0406	In control	–	–	–	–
11.	0	0.025	0.07184	In control	0	2.5	7.184	In control
12.	0.0428	0.079	0.11518	Out of control	–	–	–	–
13.	0.00378	0.1078	0.21183	In control	0.3024	8.625	16.947	In control

	C chart			
	LCL	CL	UCL	Decision
14.	0	3.1	8.3820	In control
15.	0	7.16667	15.1978	In control
16.	0	3.5	9.1125	In control
17.	0	3.6	9.2920	In control

Exercise 1 (C)

I. **Multiple Choice Questions :**
- **Choose the correct alternative out of four alternatives given below for each questions.**
    1. The minor variations in manufacturing processes are due to
        (a) chance cause
        (b) assignable cause
        (c) both (a) and (b)
        (c) neither (a) nor (b)

2. The process is said to be under statistical control if
   (a) R chart is in control, $\bar{X}$ chart is not in control
   (b) R chart is out of control, $\bar{X}$ chart is under control
   (c) both charts are under control
   (d) none of the charts are under control
3. R chart is used to control the variation
   (a) within the subgroups   (b) between the subgroups
   (c) both within and between   (d) between the operators
4. The process standard deviation is estimated by
   (a) $\bar{\bar{X}}$ (b) $\bar{R}$ (c) $\bar{R}/d_2$ (d) $\bar{R}/D_2$
5. The control lines are :
   (a) always equidistant from central line
   (b) equidistant from central line in case of $\bar{X}$ chart
   (c) equidistant from central line in case of R chart
   (d) equidistant from central line if the process is under statistical control
6. Points falling above UCL is indication of
   (a) increase in variation
   (b) increase in mean
   (c) presence of some assignable cause
   (d) presence of some chance cause
7. In $\bar{X}$ chart the control limits are
   (a) $\mu \pm 3\sigma$ (b) $\bar{\bar{X}} \pm 3\bar{R}/d_2$
   (c) $\bar{\bar{X}} \pm 3A_2\bar{R}$ (d) $\bar{\bar{X}} \pm 3A_1\bar{R}$
8. If the manufacturing process is under statistical control then
   (a) it meets specification
   (b) it may not meet specifications
   (c) it produces, zero defective items
   (d) it meets specification if the process standard deviation is very small
9. In order draw R chart we take
   (a) LCL = $D_1\bar{R}$, UCL = $D_2\bar{R}$
   (b) LCL = $d_1\bar{R}$, UCL = $d_2\bar{R}$
   (c) UCL = $\bar{R} + D_1\bar{R}$, LCL = $\bar{R} - D_1\bar{R}$
   (d) LCL = $D_3\bar{R}$, UCL = $D_4\bar{R}$

10. If $\bar{\bar{X}} = 50$, $\bar{R} = 1$, $d_2 = 2.326$ for $n = 5$ then

   (a) $\hat{\mu} = 50$, $\hat{\sigma} = 1$

   (b) $\hat{\mu} = \dfrac{50}{2.326}$, $\hat{\sigma} = 2.326$

   (c) $\hat{\mu} = \dfrac{50}{\sqrt{5}}$, $\hat{\sigma} = \dfrac{1}{\sqrt{5}}$

   (d) $\hat{\mu} = 50$, $\hat{\sigma} = \dfrac{1}{2.326}$

11. The LCL and UCL of p chart are given by

   (a) $\bar{p} - 3\sqrt{\dfrac{\bar{p}\bar{q}}{n}}$, $\bar{p} + 3\sqrt{\dfrac{\bar{p}\bar{q}}{n}}$

   (b) $\bar{p} - \dfrac{3\sqrt{\bar{p}\bar{q}}}{n}$, $\bar{p} + \dfrac{3\sqrt{\bar{p}\bar{q}}}{n}$

   (c) $\bar{p} - 3A_2\sqrt{\bar{p}\bar{q}}$, $\bar{p} + 3A_2\sqrt{\bar{p}\bar{q}}$

   (d) $\bar{p} - \sqrt{\dfrac{3\bar{p}\bar{q}}{n}}$, $\bar{p} + \sqrt{\dfrac{3\bar{p}\bar{q}}{n}}$

12. The LCL and UCL of C chart are given by

   (c) $\bar{C} - 3\sqrt{\bar{C}}$, $\bar{C} + 3\sqrt{\bar{C}}$

   (b) $\bar{C} - \sqrt{3\bar{C}}$, $\bar{C} + \sqrt{3\bar{C}}$

   (c) $\bar{C} - \dfrac{\sqrt{\bar{C}}}{3}$, $\bar{C} + \dfrac{\sqrt{\bar{C}}}{3}$

   (d) $\dfrac{\bar{C} - \sqrt{\bar{C}}}{3}$, $\dfrac{\bar{C} + \sqrt{\bar{C}}}{3}$

13. We use C chart when
   (a) the characteristics is a variable.
   (b) the characteristics is a attribute by classification as defective or good.
   (c) the number of defects per unit are counted.
   (d) the number of defectives in a lost is counted.

14. We use p chart when
   (a) the characteristics is a variable.
   (b) the characteristics is a attribute by classification as defective or good.
   (c) the number of defects per unit are counted.
   (d) the number of defectives in a lost is counted.

15. We use $\bar{X}$-R chart when
   (a) the characteristics is a variable.
   (b) the characteristics is a attribute by classification as defective or good.
   (c) the number of defects per unit are counted.
   (d) the number of defectives in a lost is counted.

II. State True or False :

16. Variation due to assignable causes is avoidable.
17. Variation within group is due to chances causes.
18. If all the points on control chart lie within LCL and UCL the process is under statistical control.
19. If process is within control, then there is no defective items produced.
20. The control limits on R chart are equidistant from control line.

III. Fill in the Blanks :

21. Using control chart we can find ...... cause of variation,.
22. If the characteristics is ...... in nature we use $\bar{X}$-R chart.
23. The LCL, UCL of $\bar{X}$-R chart are ......
24. The LCL, UCL of P chart are ......
25. The LCL, UCL of C chart are ......

Answers 1(C)

I. Multiple Choice Questions :

(1) a (2) c (3) a (4) d
(5) b (6) c (7) c (8) b
(9) d (10) d (11) a (12) a
(13) c (14) d (15) a

II. True or False :

(16) True (17) True (18) False (19) False
(20) False

III. Fill in the Blanks :

(21) Assignable (22) Variable (23) $D_3\bar{R}, D_4\bar{R}, \bar{X} \pm A_2\bar{R}$

(24) $\bar{P} \pm 3\sqrt{\dfrac{\bar{p}\bar{q}}{n}}$ (25) $\bar{C} \pm 3\sqrt{\bar{C}}$

Chapter 2...

Index Numbers

Contents ...

2.1 Introduction
2.2 Definition and Notation of Index Number
2.3 Types of Index Numbers
2.4 Construction of Index Numbers
2.5 Cost of Living Index Numbers
2.6 Use of Cost of Living Index Numbers
2.7 Commonly used Index Numbers in India

Key Words :

Prices, Quantities, Current Year, Base Year, Price Relatives, Index Numbers, Weight, Laspeyre's Index Number, Paasche's Index Number, Fisher's Index Number, Cost of Living Index Numbers, Family Budget Method, Aggregate Expenditure Method, Inflation, Cost Inflation Index.

Objectives :

To built-up a tool to measure the average changes in prices and to use it for various financial and economic activities. Index numbers are often called as economic barometer.

2.1 Introduction

Index number is a tool used to measure the changes in prices of commodities, industrial and mineral production, sales, imports, exports etc. It was first developed by an Italian economist Mr. Carli, in 1764, for comparison of prices of commodities. Index number serves the purpose of economic indicators. The fields in which index numbers are used are economics, trade, stock market, Government organisations etc. The popularly used index numbers are

    (i)   Bombay Stock Exchange (BSE) SENSEX index number.
    (ii)   National Stock Exchange (NSE) index numbers.
    (iii) All India wholesale price index number.
    (iv) Consumer price index numbers.
    (v)   Index number of Industrial Production (1993-94 as base year).
    (vi) Index numbers of agricultural production.
    (vii) Cost inflation index (for capital assets).

Index Number - An Economic Barometer : (April 2009)

Economic phenomena are dynamic, we observe that the prices of commodities change from time to time, place to place, wages of workers, prices of shares, exhibit up and down movements, industrial production also undergoes changes. Index numbers measure such changes, infact they measure pulse of economy like inflationary or deflationary tendencies. The apparatus barometer reflects the changes in atmospheric pressure likewise, index numbers reflects the changes in economic activities; hence index numbers are rightly called as **'economic barometers'**.

For the determination of index numbers, we need to consider several commodities. We know that a series of observations can be reduced to a single observation or two series can be compared with the help of averages. Thus, it is essential to find the average change in prices or quantities to find index numbers. But to calculate an average, we require the observations measured in same units. However, the prices and quantities differ in their units.

For example, prices of sugar, rice are expressed in ₹ per kg. whereas prices of milk, petrol etc. are in ₹ per litre, price of cloth is ₹ per metre. Thus, average of prices of such quantities is meaningless and it no longer remains useful. In order to overcome this difficulty, changes are measured in ratios, which are unitless numbers and then average change is calculated. The average so obtained is an index number. Thus, index number is an elegant application of measures of central tendency.

2.2 Definition and Notation of Index Numbers (April 2010, 2011)

Definition : Index number is a number designated to measure the average change in the values of a **group of related variables** over two different **situations**.

The group of variables may be prices of specified commodities, quantities of industrial production, volume of imports, exports etc. Two different situations may be two different times or places.

Problems or considerations in the Construction of Index Numbers

The various problems involved in the construction of index numbers are discussed below :

1. Purpose of Index Number : The purpose for which the index number is constructed should be clearly and unambiguously mentioned. Similarly, the scope of index number should also be defined clearly. *For example*, if we want to construct a consumer's price index numbers, accordingly appropriate commodities are to be selected. Similarly, a class of people for which the index number is to be constructed should be clearly stated. Thus, defining the purpose clearly, helps in selection of commodities, base period, weights etc.

2. Selection of Commodities : Selection of commodities is an important factor in the construction of index numbers. There are no rigid rules regarding selection of commodities. Number of commodities should not be too large or too small. Inclusion of large number of commodities results into greater expenses, more time, more volume of work. If number of commodities is too small, the associated index number will not remain proper representative. Thus, a reasonable number of commodities should be included. Moreover, commodities selected should be relevant to the purpose of index number. These should be representative of tastes, customs and necessities of group of population for which index number is constructed.

For example, if we want to find the cost of living index number for poor families, then we should not include luxury goods like cars, washing machines, refrigerators, cell phones etc. Stable commodities are to be selected.

3. Collection of Data : Data may be price quotations or quantity consumed or quantity produced or quantity imported etc. depending upon the purpose of index numbers. The data should be collected from reliable agencies, standard trade journals, periodical reports, official publications etc. The data collected should be accurate and proper representative. For consumer's price index numbers, price quotations should be collected from trusted agencies. Prices vary from place to place, shop to shop and quality to quality. Therefore, prices should be collected with utmost care. As per requirement, retail or wholesale prices should be collected. Sometimes price may be quoted as number of ₹ per unit quantity.

For example, ₹ 10 per kg. On the other hand, price may be quoted as quantity per ₹ *For example*, 100 gm per Re. Price quotations should be of the same type.

4. Choice of Base Period : Index number uses two time periods. In this situation, a period for which index number is determined is called as **current period** and the period of comparison or with respect to which index number is determined is called as **base period.** The base period should be a period for which reliable figures are available. A period of economic importance may be preferably chosen. Following are the guidelines for the selection of base period :

(i) **The base period should be a normal period.** It means that there should not be incidents like war, floods, famine, earthquakes, labour strikes etc. It can be noticed that for the years with above stated abnormal conditions, economic instability will be observed, hence proper price quotations or quantity consumed, production figures may not be available.

(ii) **The base period should not be too distant.** The customs, habits, tastes of people change gradually. Hence, for proper comparison, base period should not be too distant. Sometimes in the meanwhile some old commodities get out of use and new commodities get introduced.

(iii) **The base period should not be too small or too large.** If base period is too short (for example, a single day), the prices are highly unstable. On the other hand, if the period is too large (for example, five years) then prices undergo many variations. Therefore, to get reliable price quotations, period should be of adequate length.

(iv) Sometimes base year is taken as average of many years. For example, Index number of agricultural production is with a triannual average of years 1979-82 as base year determined by Government of Maharashtra.

5. Selection of Type of Average : It is stated above that the index number is a average change in the prices or quantities. In order to combine the data, we need to use appropriate measure of central tendency. Arithmetic mean is suitable in most of the situations since it is a simple and good average. Sometimes geometric mean or median is also used.

6. Selection of Weights : Weighted average is more appropriate than simple average. Weight is a device of giving due or proper importance to the commodity. If weights are not attached, all commodities are regarded equally important. Since changes in prices of different commodities will have different influence on average, weights are essential.

For example, increase in price of salt, and that of wheat will have different influence on index number. Weight plays the role of frequency, however weights can be fractional in nature. Thus, to get true reflection of changes, weighted average is used.

(i) **Quantity weights (q)** : Amount of commodity consumed or produced or exported etc. is taken as weight.

(ii) **Value weights (V)** : It is a product of price and quantity used or produced.

Note : If $x_1, x_2, \ldots, x_n$ are the observations with weights $w_1, w_2, \ldots w_n$ respectively then weighted arithmetic mean is given by

$$\bar{X}_w = \frac{w_1 x_1 + w_2 x_2 + \ldots + w_n x_n}{w_1 + w_2 + \ldots + w_n} = \frac{\sum w \cdot x}{\sum w}$$

2.3 Types of Index Numbers

Mainly there are three types of index numbers in use viz. price index numbers, quality index numbers and value index numbers.

Price Index Numbers : Price index numbers are computed to measure the relative changes in prices of group of commodities or a single commodity. Government of India regularly computes two series of price index numbers (i) wholesale price index numbers, (ii) consumer price index numbers. Bombay stock exchange (BSE) SENSEX and NSE are two important price index numbers used in stock market to measure the changes in prices of shares.

Quantity Index Numbers : Quantity index numbers are constructed to measure the changes in volume of industrial production, agricultural production, mineral production, import, export etc.

Value Index Number : Value index number is designed to measure the percent change in aggregate expenditure for a given period.

Construction of Index Numbers

Base year is denoted by 0 and current year by 1, price and quantities are denoted by p and q respectively. Hence, value $v = p \cdot q$. Weights are represented by w. Price index number, quantity index number and value index number are denoted by P, Q and V respectively.

Thus,

p_0 : Price of a commodity in the base year.

p_1 : Price of a commodity in the current year.

q_0 : Quantity of a commodity in the base year.

q_1 : Quantity of a commodity in the current year.

P_{01} : Price index number for the current period 1 with base period 0.

Q_{01} : Quantity index number for the current period 1 with base period 0.

There are two types of index numbers (1) Aggregative type (2) Average of price relative type. Further each of these type are classified into two categories (a) Simple and (b) Weighted, thus it gives rise to four types of index numbers :

(i) Simple (unweighted) aggregative index number.

(ii) Weighted aggregative index number.

(iii) Simple average of price relatives

(iv) Weighted average of price relatives.

The following tree diagram summarizes the types of index numbers.

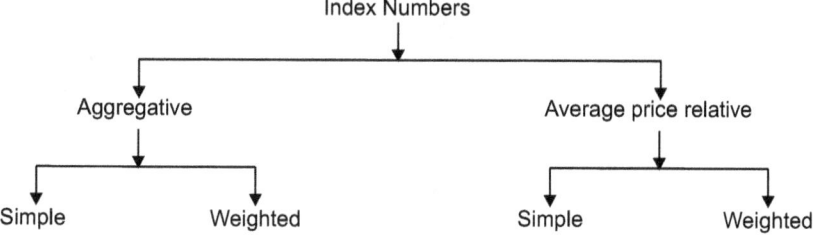

In this book, we discuss only the first two types of aggregative index numbers.

(A) Unweighted or simple aggregative type index numbers :

This type of price index number is given by

$$P_{01} = \frac{\text{Sum of prices in current year}}{\text{Sum of prices in base year}} \times 100 = \frac{\sum p_1}{\sum p_0} \times 100$$

Similarly, quantity index number is

$$Q_{01} = \frac{\sum q_1}{\sum q_0} \times 100$$

Limitations :

1. The main limitation of unweighted index numbers is, that all the commodities are given equal importance which is not the reality.

2. In aggregative type index number, $\sum p_1$ or $\sum p_0$ cannot be computed meaningfully if the units are not same. For example, some price quotations may be ₹ per kg, same may be ₹ per litre or ₹ per metre etc. Sum of such prices is not meaningful.

(B) Weighted aggregative type index numbers :

If w is the weight attached with commodity, then this type of price index number is given by,

$$P_{01} = \frac{\sum p_1 w}{\sum p_0 w} \times 100$$

and quantity index number is given by

$$Q_{01} = \frac{\sum q_1 w}{\sum q_0 w} \times 100$$

Note : In aggregative type price index numbers, quantities consumed are taken as weights and in quantity index numbers, prices are taken as weights.

Example 2.1 : *Compute price index for 2007 with 2008 as base year using simple aggregate method, for the data given below :*

Commodities	A	B	C	D	E
Price in 2006	40	60	20	50	80
Price in 2007	50	60	30	64	104

Solution :

Commodity	Price in 2006 p_0	Price in 2007 p_1
A	40	50
B	60	60
C	20	30
D	50	64
E	80	104
Total	$250 = \sum p_0$	$308 = \sum p_1$

Simple aggregate of price index number

$$P_{01} = \frac{\sum p_1}{\sum p_0} \times 100 = \frac{308}{250} \times 100 = 123.20$$

Interpretation : $P_{01} = 123.2$ means there is on an average the rise of 23.2% in prices in the year 2007 as compared to those in the year 2006.

2.4 Construction of Index Numbers

According to different weighing systems, different index numbers are obtained. We study some important index numbers below.

Some Specific Index Numbers

(A) Laspeyre's Index Number : It is a weighted aggregative type index number defined by French economist Laspeyre in the year 1871. For price index number, we take quantities of base year (q_0) as weights. Hence, Laspeyre's price index number is

$$P_{01}^L = \frac{\sum p_1 q_0}{\sum p_0 q_0} \times 100$$

Application : Cost of living index number is a Laspeyre's price index number.

(B) Paasche's Index Number : It is a price index number by German Statistician Paasche which was defined in the year 1874, we take current year quantities (q_1) as weights, thus we get

$$P_{01}^P = \frac{\sum p_1 q_1}{\sum p_0 q_1} \times 100$$

Application : To find real gross domestic product (GDP) of a country, the effect of inflation is removed by GDP deflator. GDP deflator is given by Paasche's price index number. GDP is used to compute national income.

Comparison between Laspeyre's and Paasche's Index Numbers :

1. The main drawback of Laspeyre's index number is that it suffers from upward bias. In other words, index number overestimates the value.

   On the other hand, Paasche's index number suffers from a downward bias. It underestimates the index number.

2. Paasche's index number requires more data to be collected as compared to Laspeyre's index number.

   Paasche's index number uses current year quantity as weights. Therefore, data for current year have to be collected. If we want to construct index number for 10 different years with the same base year, then we require to collect quantities for each of these 10 years. Thus, data collection work increases. Whereas Laspeyre's formula uses base year quantities, hence one set of quantities is enough for those 10 years.

3. Paasche's index number requires more calculations. If Paasche's formula is used to calculate index number for 10 different years, we need to compute denominator $\sum p_0 q_1$ for each year separately, whereas in Laspeyre's formula the denominator $\sum p_0 q_0$ calculated once will be sufficient for remaining years.

(C) Irving Fisher's Ideal Index Number : It is defined as positive square root of product of Laspeyre's and Paasche's index numbers. Thus, Fisher's price index number defined in the year 1920 is given by,

$$P_{01}^F = \sqrt{P_{01}^L \times P_{01}^P} = \sqrt{\frac{\sum p_1 q_0}{\sum p_0 q_0} \times \frac{\sum p_1 q_1}{\sum p_0 q_1}} \times 100$$

Remarks :

1. Fisher's index number uses quantities in both the years, current year as well as base year, therefore, it is superior to Laspeyre's and Paasche's index numbers.
2. Fisher's index number satisfies the tests of index numbers, which is a good index number is supposed to satisfy. Hence, it is called as ideal index number.
3. Fisher's index number is difficult to calculate as compared to Laspeyre's and Paasche's index numbers.
4. Fisher's index number lies between Laspeyre's and Paasche's index numbers. Since it is a geometric mean of Laspeyre's and Paasche's index numbers.

Example 2.2 : *Calculate price index numbers for the following data for the year 2007 taking 2006 as base year using the following formulae.*

(i) Laspeyre's, (ii) Paasche's, (iii) Fisher's.

Commodity	Year 2006		Year 2007	
	Price	Quantity	Price	Quantity
A	20	8	40	6
B	50	10	60	5
C	40	15	50	10
D	20	20	20	15

Solution :

Commodity	p_0	q_0	p_1	q_1	$p_0 q_0$	$p_1 q_1$	$p_0 q_1$	$p_1 q_0$
A	20	8	40	6	160	240	120	320
B	50	10	60	5	500	300	250	600
C	40	15	50	10	600	500	400	750
D	20	20	20	15	400	300	300	400
Total	–	–	–	–	1660	1340	1070	2070

(i) Laspeyre's price index number

$$P_{01}^L = \frac{\sum p_1 q_0}{\sum p_0 q_0} \times 100 = \frac{2070}{1660} \times 100 = 124.6988$$

(ii) Paasche's price index number

$$P_{01}^P = \frac{\sum p_1 q_1}{\sum p_0 q_1} \times 100 = \frac{1340}{1070} \times 100 = 125.2336$$

(iii) Fisher's price index number

$$P_{01}^F = \sqrt{P_{01}^L \times P_{01}^P} = 124.9659$$

Remark : It can be noticed that the different formulae of index number give different values for the same data, however, they do not vary to large extent numerically. Ideally, every formulae should give the same value.

Interpretation : The above illustration computes price index number for 2007 with a base year 2006. Here Laspeyre's price index number is 124.6988. It can be interpreted as that the average of prices in the year 2007 is 124.6988 when it was assumed to be 100 in the year 2006. Thus, the prices have increased on an average by 24.6988%.

Uses of Index Numbers : (April 2010)

1. **Index Number as a Economic Barometer :** Index numbers are useful in measuring the changes in prices, production, import, export, stock market etc. Cost of inflation index number helps us to know the appreciation of assets.
   With the help of index numbers, the changes can be quantitatively determined to a considerable accuracy. R.G.D. Allen rightly pointed out that the range of index number is quite large and they can indicate the changes in various variables such as shipping, freights, commodity prices, security prices, volume of output, profit, sales etc.

2. **Index Number helps in Comparison :** Index number helps in comparing the economic, and business activities for two different locations or periods or countries.

3. **Index Number helps in Planning and Policy Making :** Index numbers give the basis for planning it helps in policy making. For example, investments in stock market.

4. **Index Number** helps in finding Real Income or Purchasing power of money.

5. **Dearness Allowances :** Index numbers are used to fix dearness allowances of employees for adjusting the inflations.

6. Real capital gain in the sales of assets such as land, house, gold, jewellery, machinery, shares etc. can be determined using the cost inflation index numbers.

7. Index number gives the progress of industry, trends in stock markets.

8. Index number helps in finding real GDP or net national product, which is the main component in national income.

9. **Measure of inflation :** Using index number, rate of inflation can be obtained.

$$\text{Inflation} = \frac{\text{Current price index number} - \text{Previous price index number}}{\text{Previous year index number}} \times 100$$

Limitations of Index Numbers :

1. **Sampling Error :** The data used to construct an index number is obtained by method of sampling. Therefore, index numbers are subject to sampling errors.

2. **Disregard to Change in Quantity :** Consumption pattern depends upon the habits and tastes of people which change gradually. *For example*, if people tend towards the use of superior quality of commodity, prices of concerned commodity will be higher and gives higher price index. The increase is not due to increase in price but due to changes in habits. Therefore, index number becomes less reliable.

3. **Subjectivity in Base Year :** Index number requires base to be a normal period. But a person may choose a base period which is suitable for him. Thus, there may be a subjectivity in selection of base period.

4. **Limited Scope :** Scope of index number is limited to its purpose. For example, consumer price index number for urban area cannot be used for rural area.

5. Index number suffers from the drawbacks of the average that is used in construction.

6. Drawback of the formula used for the construction of index number affects its value.

7. If value index number shows an increase, then whether it is due to increase in prices or increase in production or both cannot be ascertained.

Example 2.3 : *Suppose in Dec. 1995 land was purchased at cost ₹50,000. It was sold at cost ₹1,50,000 in Feb. 2002. Find the real capital gain if the cost of inflation index in 1995-96 is 281 and that in 2001-02 is 426.*

Solution : Suppose the rise in cost is proportional to index

$$\therefore \frac{\text{Cost in 2001-02}}{\text{Cost inflation index number in 2001-02}} = \frac{\text{Cost in 1995-96}}{\text{Cost inflation index number in 1995-96}}$$

$$\therefore \text{Indexed cost in 2001-02} = \text{Cost in 1995-96} \times \frac{\text{Index number in 2001-02}}{\text{Index number in 1995-96}}$$

$$= 50{,}000 \times \frac{426}{281} = 75{,}800.71 \ ₹$$

$$\therefore \text{Capital gain} = \text{Sale price} - \text{Indexed cost}$$

$$= 1{,}50{,}000 - 75800.71 = 74{,}199.29 \ ₹$$

$$\text{Apparent gain} = \text{Sale price} - \text{Purchase price}$$

$$= 1{,}50{,}000 - 50{,}000 = 1{,}00{,}000 \ ₹$$

Thus the apparent gain is ₹ 1,00,000 however, taking into account inflation the gain in real sense is ₹ 74,199.29. For tax calculations, real capital gain is used.

Example 2.4 : *Calculate price index number using : (i) Laspeyre's, (ii) Paasche's (iii) Fishers Method for the following data :* (April 2010)

Years Commodiites	1980		1985	
	Price	Quantity	Price	Quantity
Rice	3	5	4.5	6
Cocount Oil	24	2	18	3
Tea	20	1	35	2
Washing Powder	10	4	16	4
Sugar	3.5	4	6	5

Solution :

Commodites	p_0	q_0	p_1	q_1	$p_0 q_0$	$p_0 q_1$	$p_1 q_0$	$p_1 q_1$
Rice	3	5	4.5	6	15	18	22.5	27
Coconut oil	24	2	18	3	48	72	36	54
Tea	20	1	35	2	20	40	35	70
Washing powder	10	4	16	4	40	40	64	64
Sugar	3.5	4	6	5	14	17.5	24	30
Total	–	–	–	–	137	187.5	181.5	245

(i) Laspeyre's price I. No. $= \dfrac{\Sigma p_1 q_0}{\Sigma p_0 q_0} \times 100 = \dfrac{181.5}{137} \times 100 = 132.48$

(ii) Paasche's price I. No. $= \dfrac{\Sigma p_1 q_1}{\Sigma p_0 q_1} \times 100 = \dfrac{245}{187.5} \times 100 = 130.67$

(iii) Fisher's price I. No. $= \sqrt{\text{Laspeyre's I. NO.} \times \text{Paasche's I. No.}}$
$= \sqrt{132.67 \times 130.67} = 131.57$

Example 2.5 : Calculate value index number of the following data :

Solution :

Commodity	Base Year		Current Year		$p_0 q_0$	$p_1 q_1$
	Price p_0	Quantity q_0	Price p_1	Quantity q_1		
A	8	50	10	60	400	600
B	10	40	12	50	400	600
C	5	100	8	120	500	960
D	6	300	9	250	1800	2250
Total	–	–	–	–	3100	4410

Value index number is,

$$V_{01} = \dfrac{\Sigma p_1 q_1}{\Sigma p_0 q_0} \times 100$$

$$= \dfrac{4410}{3100} \times 100 = 142.2581$$

2.5 Commonly Used Index Numbers in India

1. Index Number of Industrial Production in India (IIP) : The index number of industrial production (IIP) serves the purpose of measure of industrial growth in country. It is published by Central Statistical Organisation (CSO) for all India as a monthly series, yearly series. The base year is 1993-94.

Year	1996-97	97-98	98-99	99-2000	00-01	01-02	02-03	03-04	04-05	05-06	06-07
IIP	130.8	139.5	145.2	154.9	162.5	164.9	176.6	189.0	204.2	221.5	247.1

IIP is a weighted index number with three major groups.

Group	Mining	Manufacturing	Electricity	Total
Weight	10.47	79.36	10.17	100

Manufacturing is subdivided into 17 subgroups. Those are listed with weights in brackets used to compute IIP.

(1) Food (9.08), (2) Beverages (2.38), (3) Cotton textile (5.52), (4) Wool, silk textiles (2.26), (5) Jute textile (0.59), (6) Textile product (2.54), (7) Wood, Agriculture (2.70), (8) Paper and printing (2.65), (9) Leather (1.14), (10) Chemical (14), (11) Rubber, plastic petrolium, coal (5.73), (12) Non-metallic minerals (4.4), (13) Basic metal and alloys (7.45), (14) Metal products (2.81), (15) Machinery and equipment (9.57), (16) Transport equipments (3.98), (17) Other manufacturing industries (2.56).

Monthly index of industrial production is a weighted average of quantity relatives. Weights are proportional to the value-added in the base year. Monthly indices for sugar, tea and salt are adjusted for seasonality. Seasonal indices are determined using the method moving averages. Simple average of monthly indices is the annual index.

2. All India Wholesale Price Index Number : The Wholesale Price Index Number (WPI) is the most widely used index in business, industry and Government. The office of Economic Advisor to Govt. of India publishes WPI. The annual rate of change in WPI is interpreted as the annual rate of inflation. It is taken to be an important indicator of micro-economic stability in the economy. It is a weighted index number with base year 1993-94. There was a sharp increase in WPI in the year 2000-01 as much as 7.13%. It was due to rise in petroleum, LPG gas, Kerosene etc. in September 2000. There are 3 major subgroups.

(i) Subgroup of primary articles, contains items, food (rice, wheat etc.); cotton, jute, minerals (such as iron, mangenese). In all 80 articles are covered.

(ii) Subgroup of fuel, power, light, lubricant. It is includes 10 items.

(iii) Subgroup of manufactured articles has 270 items in it.

The group-wise weights are given below :

Subgroup	Primary articles	Fuel, power light, lubricants	Manufactured products	Total
Weight	22.025	14.226	63.749	100

WPI for years 1994-95 to 2001-02 are given below :

Year	1994-95	95-96	96-97	97-98	98-99	99-00	00-01	01-02
WPI	112.6	121.6	127.2	132.8	140.7	145.3	155.7	161.3
Year	02-03	03-04	04-05	05-06	06-07	07-08		
WPI	166.8	175.9	187.3	175.6	206.2	214.3		

3. Consumer Price Index Numbers (CPI) : Consumer Price Index (CPI) numbers are intended to measure the movements in retail prices of essential commodities for different sections of the consumers. For example,

(i) CPI for industrial workers on all India basis (also as statewise and citiwise) with a base year 1982.

(ii) CPI for urban non-mannual employees is released by CSO in monthly series on all India basis as well as regionwise and for 59 cities in country.

(iii) CPI for agricultural labours with base year 1986-87.

(iv) CPI for ubran labourers with base year 1982.

(v) CPI for rural labourers with base year with base year 1982.

All India CPI for industrial workers for 1990-91 to 2001-02 are given below :

Year	90-91	91-92	92-93	93-94	94-95	95-96	96-97	97-98	98-99	99-00	00-01	01-02
CPI	193	219	240	258	284	313	342	366	414	428	444	463
Year	02-03	03-04	04-05	05-06								
CPI	482	500	519	542								

Weights for various CP indices are as follows :

Subgroup	All India CPI for Industrial Workers	CPI for Urban Maharashtra	CPI for Rural Maharashtra
Food	57.00	54.12	61.66
Pan, Supari, Tobacco etc.	3.15	2.02	–
Fuel, power and light etc.	6.28	6.67	7.92
Clothing and bedding etc.	8.54	5.95	7.78
Housing	8.67	–	–
Miscellaneous	16.36	31.24	22.64
Total	100.00	100.00	100.00

4. Index Numbers of Agricultural Production : Index number of agricultural production for Maharashtra is calculated with triannual average base 1979-82. It is a weighted index number based five main groups (i) cereals, (ii) pulses, (iii) oil seeds, (iv) fibers and (v) miscallaneous.

Comparing index number of agricultural production for Maharashtra and all India we realise that the rate of growth in Maharashtra is less than that of in all India level. The fluctuations indicate that the agricultural production in Maharashtra is highly uncertain. In the year 2000-01 the index number is reduced by 38.5 as compared to 1999-2000 which is a substantial reduction.

Groupwise weights are as follows :

Groups	Cereals	Pulses	Oilseeds	Fibres	Miscellaneous	Total
Weights	42.22	10.44	9.16	9.93	28.25	100

The series on index number is as follows :

Year	Index No.	Year	Index No.
1982-83	97.4	1999-00	157.2
1986-87	79.7	2000-01	127.4
1990-91	136.5	2001-02	135.2
1991-92	101.4	2002-03	130.4
1992-93	134.2	2003-04	112.7
1993-94	140.3	2004-05	111.0
1994-95	136.1	2005-06	135.4
1995-96	145.7	2006-07	178.7
1996-97	160.7		
1997-98	114.5		
1998-99	156.8		

Index number of agricultural production is an important measure of economy. It has significant contribution to GDP of country. It is directly and indirectly linked with industrial sector. Fluctuations in mansoon are mainly responsible for the erratic behaviour of growth in agricultural production.

5. Security Price Indices : The Reserve Bank of India (RBI) is computing series of index numbers for security prices with base year 1980-81. Price indices are compiled weekly and the average of weeks for months or years is computed. It is presented on all India basis. For this purpose, there are 5 regions of India, viz. Mumbai, Kolkatta, Chennai, Ahmedabad, Delhi. It considers 338 actively traded shares with regional distribution as follows : Mumbai 32%, Kolkata 26%, Chennai 17%, Ahmedabad 10%, Delhi 15%. The weights are proportional to the average market value of share. A sample of securities is taken then the daily closing prices are taken into account the arithmetic mean of prices is used to compute price relatives with base year prices. The price relative of subgroup is obtained as a unweighted geometric mean of price relatives of Scrips (securities) in subgroup. Finally group indices are compiled using weighted average with weight of subgroup proportional to the number of shares outstanding in the scrip.

BSE Sensitive Index : The Bombay Stock Exchange (BSE) computes prices index since 1986, with a base year 1978-79. It is recognised as BSE sensex. It has 30 Scrips which are actively traded, many of which are in Group A (Specified group) and few are in Group B (non-specified group). These indices are available daily, monthly and yearly in leading newspapers.

BSE National Index : Bombay stock exchange also computes a series of index numbers on all India basis. It includes in all 100 Scrips out of which 22 a quoted in Mumbai only, 72 from BSE and 6 from other stock exchanges. The base year 1983-84 is chosen due to price stability and relative proximity. There are several series of security price indices. NSE is compiling since 1995 with base year 1995. It uses 50 Scrips (called as NIFTY) out of 550 listed Scrips and 1500 trades Scrips.

All these indices are security market indicators.

6. Cost Inflation Index : In order to determine the real capital gain due to the sale of assets, Government of India computes index number of cost of inflation with a base year 1981-82. It is 75% of the rise in consumer price index number for urban non-manual employees. It is used for calculation of income tax for income generated due to sales of capital assets such as land, house, gold, shares etc.

Apparently, profit = sale price − purchase price. However one has to take into account the effect of inflation. Price inflation is considered to be proportional to the cost inflation index, accordingly the indexed cost of assets is determined for the year of transaction, then

Real capital gain = Sale price − Indexed cost.

To determine indexed cost we use the following relation.

$$\frac{\text{Purchase price}}{\text{Cost of inflation index in the purchase year}} = \frac{\text{Indexed cost}}{\text{Cost of inflation index in the year of transaction}}$$

$$\therefore \text{Indexed cost} = \text{Purchase cost} \times \frac{\text{Cost inflation index in the year of transaction}}{\text{Cost inflation index in the year of purchase}}$$

The series of index of cost inflation is as follows :

Year	81-82	95-96	96-97	97-98	98-99	99-00	00-01	01-02	02-03
Cost inflation index	100	281	305	331	351	389	406	426	447
Year	03-04	04-05	05-06	06-07					
Cost inflation index	463	480	497	519					

Case Study :

An industrial visits, ABC firm of Charted Accountants. He would like to file his income tax return. He sold his land property at ₹ 5 crores in year 2007-08, it was purchased in 1991-92 at ₹ 1.5 crores. He sold shares of company at ₹ 1 crores in 2007-08, which were obtained from public issue in the year 1995-96 at ₹ 30 lacs. Chartered accountant decided to use cost inflation index number to find the real gain. Apparently his profit is ₹ 3.5 crores on land and ₹ 70 lacks from shares.

Points to Remember

1. Laspeyre's price index number = $P_{01}^L = \dfrac{\sum p_1 q_0}{\sum p_0 q_0} \times 100$

   Paasche's price index number = $P_{01}^P = \dfrac{\sum p_1 q_1}{\sum p_1 q_1} \times 100$

   Fisher's price index number = $P_{01}^F = \sqrt{P_{01}^L \times P_{01}^P}$

2. Fisher's index number numerically lies between Laspeyre's and Pasche's index number.

Exercise 2 (A)

A. Theory Questions :

1. What is meant by Index Numbers ?
2. State the uses of Index Numbers.
3. Explain how index numbers are constructed.
4. Define price relative and discuss how it is used in construction of index numbers.
5. Explain the terms : base year, current year, weight.
6. Discuss the various problems involved in the construction of index numbers.
7. Explain why index numbers are called as economic barometers.
8. Explain what precautions you will take for the selection of base period.
9. Explain the importance of weights in construction of index numbers.
10. State the limitations of index number by the method of simple aggregative.
11. Discuss the problems of
    (i) selection of commodities (ii) selection of average (iii) selection of weights (iv) collection of data (v) choise of base year in the construction of index numbers.
12. Define (i) Laspeyre's (ii) Paasche's and (iii) Fisher's index numbers.
13. Make a critical comparison between Laspeyre's and Paasche's index numbers.
14. Explain the drawbacks of each of the following index numbers :
    (i) Laspeyre's Index Number. (ii) Paasche's Index Number. (iii) Fisher's Index Number.
15. Mention the limitations of index numbers.
16. How index number is interpreted ?
17. Write a note on : (i) SENSEX, (ii) NIFTY.

Exercise 2 (B)

B. Index Number using Raw Data :

1. Calculate price index number using :
   (i) Laspeyr'es method.
   (ii) Paasche's method.
   (iii) Fisher's method from the information given below :

Item	Base Year		Current Year	
	Price	Quantity	Price	Quantity
Cheese	18	2	24	1.5
Bread	12	30	15	15
Eggs	20	15	30	15
Milk	10	30	19	25

2. Calculate price index number using :
   (i) Laspeyre's
   (ii) Paasches
   (iii) Fishers method for the following data :

Years Commodities	Base Year		Current Year	
	Price ₹	Quantity	Price ₹	Quantity
Rice	25	5	30	6
Coconut oil	60	2	100	3
Tea	100	1	120	2
Washing powder	100	4	120	4
Sugar	30	4	40	5

3. Compute Fisher's price index number for the following data :

Commodity	Base Year		Current Year	
	Quantity	Expenses	Quantity	Expenses
A	50	300	56	560
B	100	200	120	240
C	60	240	60	360
D	30	300	24	288
E	40	320	36	432

4. Compute Laspeyre's price index number for 1995 from the following data :

Commodity	Price in		Quantity in 1990
	1990	1995	
Wheat	5	7	100
Rice	10	18	60
Jowar	5	8	30
Gram	10	16	10

5. Find Laspeyre's, Paasche's and Fisher's index numbers for the following data.

Commodity	p_0	q_0	p_1	q_1
A	4	5	12	3
B	4	4	6	4
C	2	3	3	5

6. Compute Laspeyre's, Paasche's, Fisher's, price index numbers for the following data :

Commodity	Base Year		Current Year	
	Price	Quantity	Price	Quantity
A	4	6	5	4
B	5	4	6	2
C	6	2	8	1

Interpret the results.

7. Find Laspeyre's, Paasche's and Fisher's price index numbers for the following data :

Commodity	A	B	C	D
p_0	9	8	4	1
q_0	5	10	6	4
p_1	15	12	5	2
q_1	5	11	6	8

8. From the data given below, construct Laspeyre's, Paasche's and Fisher's price index numbers, also verify that Fisher's index number lies between that of Laspeyre's and Paasche's index numbers.

Commodity	2011		2012	
	Price	Quantity	Price	Quantity
A	6	50	10	56
B	2	100	2	120
C	4	60	6	60
D	10	30	12	24
E	8	20	12	36

9. Compute Laspeyre's and Paasche's price index numbers for the following data :

Commodity	p_0	q_0	p_1	q_1
A	5	8	3	4
B	2	6	6	2
C	1	5	2	3

10. Calculate Fisher's price index numbers for the following data :

Commodities	2011		2012	
	Price (₹)	Quantity (kg.)	Price (₹)	Quantity (kg.)
A	20	8	40	6
B	50	10	60	5
C	40	15	50	10
D	20	20	20	15

C. Index Number Summerised Data :

11. Given : $\sum p_1q_0 = 1900$, $\sum p_0q_0 = 1360$, $\sum p_1q_1 = 1880$, $\sum p_0q_1 = 1344$.
    Find Laspeyre's, Paasche's and Fisher's Price Index Number.
12. Given : $\sum p_1q_0 = 175$, $\sum p_0q_0 = 91$, $\sum p_1q_1 = 190$, $\sum p_0q_1 = 100$.
    Find Laspeyre's, Paasche's and Fisher's price index number.
13. If $\sum p_0q_0 = 6000$, $\sum p_0q_1 = 8000$, $\sum p_1q_0 = 9000$, $\sum p_1q_1 = 10,000$.
    Find Laspeyre's, Paasche's and Fisher's price index number.
14. If $\sum p_1 q_0 = 750$, $\sum p_1q_1 = 860$, $\sum p_0q_0 = 700$, $\sum p_0q_1 = 830$ find the price index numbers by
    (i) Laspeyre's method, (ii) Paasche's method, (iii) Fisher's method.
15. Compute the real salary of a person, if his salary in the year 2000 is ₹ 12,900 and the index number in the year 2000 is 430.

D. Missing Value Problem :

16. Find value of X if for the following data if Laspeyre's price index number is 114.4 :

Commodity	Price		Base Year Quantity
	Base Year	Current Year	
A	36	40	100
B	80	90	12
C	45	41	X
D	5	6	1100

17. Find the missing price if ratio of Laspeyre's price index to Paasche's price index is 28 : 27 for the following data :

Commodity	p_0	q_0	p_1	q_1
A	1	10	2	5
B	1	5	*	2

18. Find the value of x if Laspeyre's and Paasche's price index numbers are equal.

Commodity	p_0	q_0	p_1	q_1
A	20	80	22	x
B	14	64	18	80

Answers 2 (B)

1. 152.41, 151, 151.70
2. 128.32, 129.63, 128.98
3. 188.73
4. 161.48
5. 221.43, 197.37, 205.05
6. 125, 125, 125
7. 152.29, 153.33, 152.81
8. 138.33, 139.88, 139.10
9. 122.8, 111.11
10. 124.97
11. 139.71, 139.88, 139.80

12. 192.31, 190.00, 191.15
13. 150, 125, 136.93
14. (i) 107.14, 103.61, 105.36
15. ₹ 3000
16. 16.35
17. 4
18. 100

Exercise 2 (C)

I. Fill in the Blanks :

1. The index number of base year is ......
2. If Laspeyre's and Paasche's price indices are 121 and 100 then Fisher's index number is ......
3. If Laspeyre's and Paasche's index numbers are same and the common value is 120, then the Fisher's index number is ......
4. The Laspeyre's index number is given by ......
5. The Paasche's index number is given by ......
6. The Fisher's index number is given by ......
7. The index number are ...... barometers ......
8. The idea of index number is due to economist ......
9. The weights used in Laspeyre's index numbers are ......
10. The weights used in Paasche's index numbers are ......

II. Multiple Choice Questions :

- **Choose the correct alternatives out of four alternatives given below for each question.**

1. Index numbers measure the average
   (a) relative changes.
   (b) absolute changes.
   (c) percentage increase.
   (d) proportionate changes.
2. Base year of index number is
   (a) any convenient year.
   (b) preceeding year.
   (c) year of stability.
   (d) succeeding year.
3. Price index number needs
   (a) price in ₹ per unit.
   (b) price in fixed number of units.
   (c) quantities in same units.
   (d) no restrictions on units of either prices or quantities.

4. Laspeyre's price index number uses weight as
   (a) base year quantity.
   (b) current year quantity.
   (c) arithmetic mean of base year quantity and current year quantity.
   (d) geometric mean of current year quantity and base year quantity.
5. Paasche's price index number uses weight as
   (a) base year quantity.
   (b) current year quantity.
   (c) arithmetic mean of base year quantity and current year quantity.
   (d) geometric mean of current year quantity and base year quantity.
6. Index numbers are called as
   (a) economic thermometer.   (b) economic barometer.
   (c) social barometer.   (d) economic accelerators.
7. Laspeyre's index number suffers from
   (a) upward bias.   (b) downward bias.
   (c) either upward or downward bias.   (d) no bias.
8. Paasche's index number suffers from
   (a) upward bias.   (b) downward bias.
   (c) either upward or downward bias.   (d) no bias.
9. If Laspeyre's index number is 120 and Paasche's index number is 130, then Fisher's index number is
   (a) $\sqrt{120 \times 130}$ (b) 125
   (c) 120   (d) cannot be determined.
10. Weights used in index numbers based on average price relatives are
    (a) price weights.   (b) quantity weights.
    (c) value weights.   (d) arbitrary weights.
11. Weights used in price index numbers based on aggregative method are
    (a) price weights.   (b) quantity weights.
    (c) value weights.   (d) arbitrary weights.
12. If prices are in ₹ and quantities are in kg, then price index numbers
    (a) are unitless.   (b) are in ₹
    (c) are in ₹ per kg.   (d) percent ₹ per kg.
13. Combined changes in prices and quantities are measured by
    (a) price index number   (b) quantity index number.
    (c) value index number.   (d) none of the above.
14. If $P_{01}^L \geq P_{01}^P$, then
    (a) $P_{01}^P \leq P_{01}^F \leq P_{01}^L$ (b) $P_{01}^F \leq P_{01}^P \leq P_{01}^L$
    (c) $P_{01}^L \leq P_{01}^F \leq P_{01}^P$ (d) $P_{01}^L \leq P_{01}^P \leq P_{01}^F$

15. If $P_{01}^L = P_{01}^P$, then

    (a) $P_{01}^F > P_{01}^P$ (b) $P_{01}^F \neq P_{01}^P$

    (c) $P_{01}^P = P_{01}^F = P_{01}^L$ (d) $P_{01}^F \neq P_{01}^L$

16. If the ratio of Laspeyre's index number to Paasche's index number is 9 : 7, then the ratio of Laspeyre's index number to that of Drobish Bowley's index number is

    (a) 9 : 7   (b) 9 : 16   (c) 8 : 9   (d) 9 : 8

17. Index number of industrial production is a

    (a) price index number.   (b) value index number.

    (c) quantity index number.   (d) any of the above type.

III. State whether the following statements are True or False :

1. Index number of base year is 0.
2. Price relative is the difference between current year price and base year price.
3. Index numbers are unitless.
4. The unweighted aggregative price index numbers need the prices in the same units.
5. Inflation is measured with the help of index numbers.
6. Unweighted index numbers are superior to weighted index numbers.
7. Selection of improper base year gives misleading indices.
8. Index numbers lie between 0 to 100.
9. Real wages are wages divided by cost of living index number.
10. Consumer price index number uses only one commodity.

Answers

I. Fill in the Blanks :

1. 100 2. 110 3. 120. 4. $\frac{\sum p_1 q_0}{\sum p_0 q_0} \times 100$ 5. $\frac{\sum p_1 q_1}{\sum p_0 q_1} \times 100$ 6. $\sqrt{\frac{\sum p_1 q_0}{\sum p_0 q_0} \times \frac{\sum p_1 q_1}{\sum p_0 q_0}} \times 100$

7. Economic 8. Mr. Carli 9. base years quantity. 10. Current year quantity.

II. Multiple Choice Questions :

(1) a	(2) c	(3) d	(4) a
(5) b	(6) a	(7) a	(8) b
(9) a	(10) c	(11) b	(12) a
(13) c	(14) a	(15) c	(16) d
(17) c			

III. True or False :

(1) False	(2) False	(3) True	(4) True
(5) True	(6) False	(7) True	(8) False
(9) True	(10) False		

Chapter 3...

Probability

Contents ...

3.1 Introduction
3.2 Types of Sets
3.3 Set Operations
3.4 Set Identities
4.5 Sample Space and Events
4.6 Probability of an Event
3.7 Important Results on Probability
3.8 Independent Events.

Key Words :

Set, Types of sets, Operations on sets, Sample space, Events, Probability of events, Sure event, Impossible events, Independent events, Mutually exclusive events (disjoint events).

Objectives :

To Write the sample space and events. To express the events in set notations. To understand basic concept of probability. To compute probabilities of different events. Solve elementary numerical problems on probability.

3.1 Introduction

The notion of uncertainty or chance is very much common in day-to-day life. For example,

(a) It may rain today.

(b) A particular political party may win the election.

(c) Investment in a shares of a particular company may be profitable.

(d) An individual may survive upto age 100 years.

In order to study the phenomena involving uncertainty, probability theory is used as a tool.

It can also be noticed that uncertainty is involved in business activities, field of management, field of economics etc. It can be observed that uncertainty comes into picture if the phenomena or experiment results into two or more possibilities. For example,

(a) Recording a result of student.

(b) Drawing a card from a well shuffled pack of 52 playing cards.

(c) Observing a number on the uppermost face, on rolling a die.

(d) Number of seeds germinated out of 100 seeds sown in a plot.

In order to study probability theory we require knowledge of set theory, permutations and combinations. We summarize below set theory.

3.2 Types of Sets

Set : A *set* is defined as collection of well-defined objects.

Examples :

(a) A group of students in a particular college.

(b) A collection of books in a particular library.

(c) A collection of items manufactured by a particular machine.

(d) A collection of types of cars in a garage.

A set is represented by curly brackets which encloses the elements of set. Set is denoted by capital letter such as A, B, C …

For example : A = {1, 2, 4, 8}, B = {20, 0, – 1}, C = {x|x even integer}.

Null set or Empty set : A set without any element is called as null set or empty set. It is denoted by Greek letter ϕ (read as phi).

Example : Set of odd numbers which are divisible by 2 is a an empty set.

Universal set : A set of all elements under study is called as universal set.

Singleton set : A set containing only one element is called as singleton set.

Subset : Set A is said to be a subset of B if every element of A is also an element of B.

Moreover B is called as supper set of A. If A is subset of B we write symbolically $A \subset B$ and B is a superset of A as $B \supset A$.

Example : Let A = {1, 4, 5, 10} and B = {1, 4, 5, 10, 12}, C = {1, 10}.

Here $A \subset B, C \subset A, C \subset B$.

3.3 Set Operations

Here we mention three basic set operations viz., union, intersection and complementation.

Union of set : The union of two sets A and B is a set of elements which belong to either A or B or both A and B. We denoted symbolically A union B as $A \cup B$.

Union of three or more sets is defined in the same manner. Sets can also be represented by diagrams called as Venn diagrams. We represent below union of sets by such diagrams.

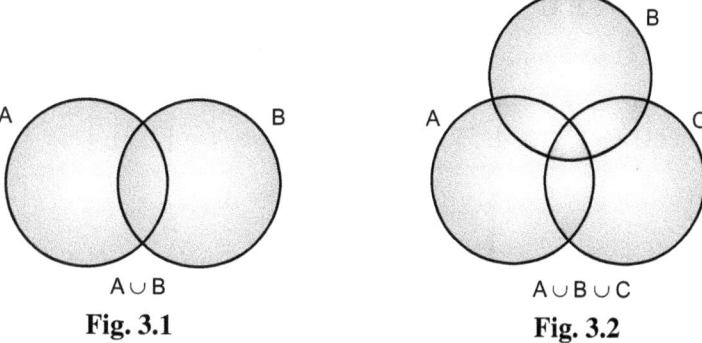

Fig. 3.1   Fig. 3.2

Example : Let A = {1, 2, 5, 7}, B = {1, 5, 7, 9} then A ∪ B = {1, 2, 5, 7, 9}.

Note : Elements common to A and B are considered only once for obtaining A ∪ B.

Intersection of sets : The intersection of two sets A and B is a set of elements which are common to both A and B. Symbolically it is denoted by A ∩ B and read as A intersection B.

Intersection of three or more sets can be defined similarly. It may be depicted by Venn diagram as follows :

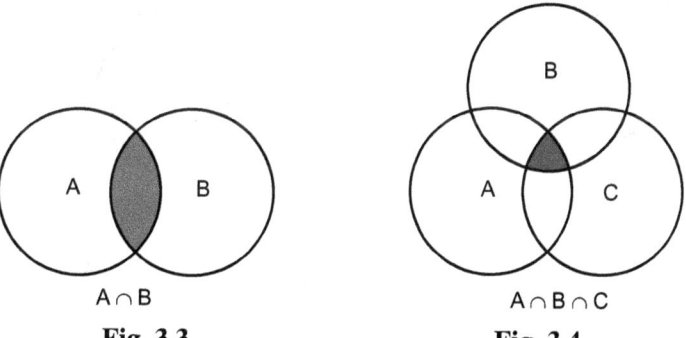

Fig. 3.3   Fig. 3.4

Disjoint sets : Two sets A and B are said to be disjoint if they have no element in common. In other words A ∩ B = φ.

Example : Let A = {1, 2, 3, 4}, B = {2, 4, 5, 6}, C = {5, 6}.

∴ A ∩ B = {2, 4}, A ∩ C = φ. Hence, A and C are disjoint sets. Whereas A and B are not disjoint.

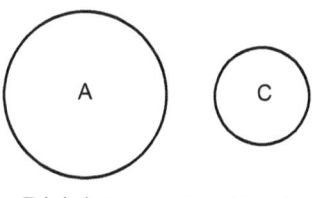

Disjoint sets, A ∩ C = φ

Fig. 3.5

Complement of set : If U is universal set and A is subset of U, then complement of A is a set of elements of U which are not in A. We denote it by A' or A^C or $\bar{A}$ and read as A complement.

Example : Let U = {1, 2, 3, 4, 5}, A = {1, 4, 5} then A' = {2, 3}.

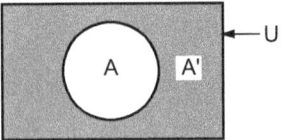

Fig. 3.6

Illustration 1 : Denote the following sets in set notation and represent those by Venn diagram. (a) A is a subset of B. (b) Set of elements of A but not B. (c) Set of elements of B but not A. (d) Set of elements of neither A nor B. (e) Set of elements of either A or B. (f) Set of elements of A and B but not C. (g) Set of elements of A and B and C.

Solution :

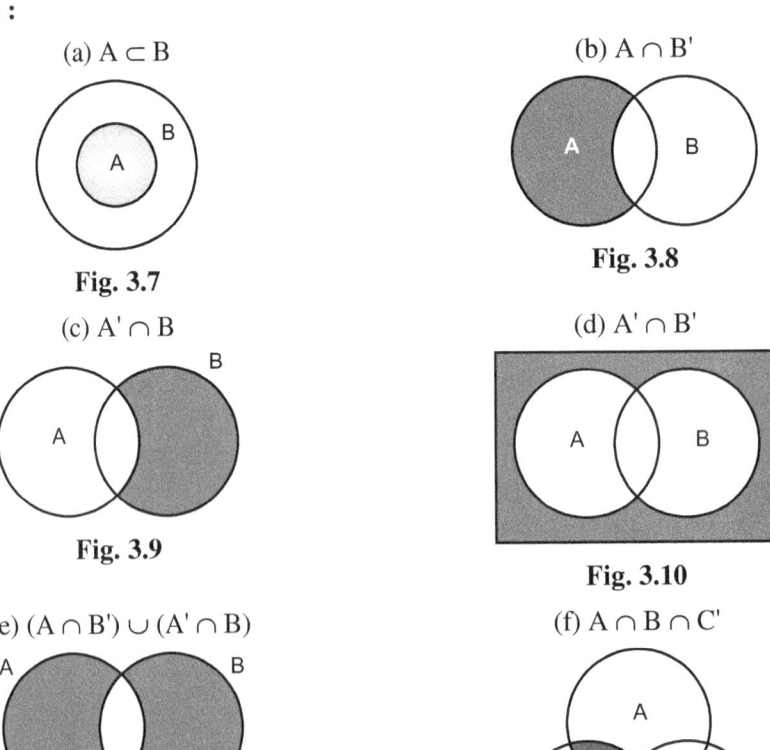

(g) $A \cap B \cap C$

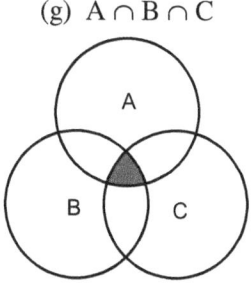

Fig. 3.13

3.3 Set Identities

(a) Commutativity : $A \cup B = B \cup A$, $A \cap B = B \cap A$

(b) De Morgan's laws : $(A \cup B)' = A' \cap B'$, $(A \cap B)' = A' \cap B'$

One can clearly note the following results $A \cap \phi = \phi$, $A \cap A = A$, $(A')' = A$, if $A \subset B$ then $A \cap B = A$. Similarly $A \cup \phi = A$, $A \cup A = A$ if $A \subset B$ then $A \cup B = B$.

3.4 Sample Space and Events

Consider the case of examination result of a student selected at random, there are two possibilities viz. pass, fail. We cannot tell in advance which possibility or outcome will occur. Moreover outcome is random or uncertain that is, it cannot be predicted with certainty. However, to determine the outcome we need to wait till results are declared. The process of obtaining outcome is called as *experiment*. If there are several outcomes associated with a phenomenon and outcomes are random, the corresponding experiment is called as *random experiment*.

Sample space : The set of all possible distinct outcomes of an experiment is called a *sample space*.

Sample space is denoted by S or Greek letter Ω (read as omega). It is nothing but universal set concerned with the experiment.

Elements of Ω are denoted by $e_1, e_2, ..., e_n$.

Hence, Ω or $S = \{e_1, e_2, e_3, ..., e_n\}$.

The elements of sample space are different outcomes which are called as *sample points*.

To illustrate the concept of sample space we discuss below few examples :

1. Consider an experiment of tossing a coin. The corresponding sample space will be

$$\Omega = \{Head, Tail\} = \{H, T\}$$

Head   Tail

Fig. 3.14 (a)

2. Consider an experiment of tossing two coins.

   Then   Ω = {HH, HT, TH, TT}

3. Suppose a die is rolled and the number on uppermost face is noted then

   Ω = {1, 2, 3, 4, 5, 6}

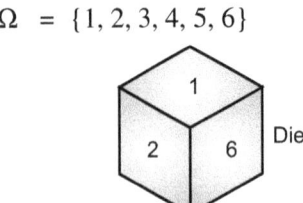

Fig. 3.14 (b)

4. Suppose a pair of dice is rolled and the number on the uppermost faces are noted then,

$$\Omega = \begin{Bmatrix} (1,1), (1,2), \ldots, (1,6) \\ (2,1), (2,2), \ldots, (2,6) \\ (3,1), (3,2), \ldots, (3,6) \\ (4,1), (4,2), \ldots, (4,6) \\ (5,1), (5,2), \ldots, (5,6) \\ (6,1), (6,2), \ldots, (6,6) \end{Bmatrix}$$

5. If a card is drawn from a well-shuffled pack of playing cards and suit is recorded, then

   Ω = {Hearts, Spades, Diamonds, Clubs} = { ♥, ♠, ♦, ♣}.

6. If a card is drawn from a well-shuffled pack of playing cards and denomination is noted, then

   Ω = {Ace, 2, 3, 4, 5, 6, 7, 8, 9, 10, jack, queen, king)

7. Student appears for an examination till he passes it

   then   Ω = {P, FP, FFP, FFFP, ...)

Event : A subset of a sample space is called as an *event*.

Event is denoted by capital letter such as A, B, C, ... etc. We say event A has occurred if the outcome belongs to set A. We give below the examples to clarify the meaning of event.

Examples :

1. Consider experiment of tossing two coins then, event A : Occurrence of single head can be written as A = {HT, TH}.

   Corresponding to Ω : {HH$_1$, TH$_1$, HT$_1$, TT}

2. In an experiment of rolling a die, let

   Event A : Getting odd number on the uppermost

   i.e.   A = {1, 3, 5}

   Event B : Getting a number multiple of three on the uppermost face.

   i.e.   B = {3, 6}

3. In an experiment of rolling two dice let,

   Event   A = Getting sum of 10 of the numbers on uppermost faces
                  = {(6, 4), (5, 5), (4, 6)}
                B = Getting sum 13 of the numbers on uppermost faces
                  = { } = ϕ

Types of events : According to the nature of set, types of events are defined. We discuss below different types of events.

1. Elementary event or Simple event : An event containing only one element is called as *elementary event* or *simple event*. In other words a singleton set is called as elementary event.

For example : An event A getting a number multiple of 5 on uppermost face of a rolled die, hence A = {5}.

2. Impossible event : An event corresponding to empty set is called as an *impossible event*. In other words an event which does not contain any sample point is called as an impossible event.

For example : If a single coin is tossed then getting two heads is an impossible event.

3. Sure event or Certain event : An event containing all sample points of Ω is called a *sure event* or *certain event*. In other words an event corresponding to the entire sample space Ω is called as a sure event.

For example : In an experiment of rolling a die getting a number either even or odd on uppermost face is a certain event or sure event.

4. Complement of an event : If A is an event on Ω then A' is called as *complement of event A*.

For example : In an experiment of rolling a die, A : Occurrence of odd number on uppermost face and B : Occurrence of even number on uppermost face are complementary events of each other.

Similarly impossible event and sure events are complements of each other.

5. Mutually exclusive or Disjoint events : Events A and B of sample space Ω are said to be mutually exclusive if $A \cap B = \phi$.

For example : In an experiment of drawing a card from well shuffled pack of playing cards let, A = Occurrence of red card B = Occurrence of black card.

Clearly,

$A \cap B = \phi$, hence A and B are mutually exclusive.

Similarly, events A, B, C are said to be mutually exclusive if $A \cap B \cap C = \phi$.

Clearly A and A' are mutually exclusive.

6. Exhaustive events : Events A and B of Ω said to be exhaustive if $A \cup B = \Omega$. In general, the events $A_1, A_2, ..., A_n$ are said to be exhaustive if,

$A_1 \cup A_2 \cup ... \cup A_n = \Omega$.

For example : If $\Omega = \{1, 2, 3, 4, 5, 6\}$

$A_1 = \{1, 3\}, A_2 = \{2, 5\}, A_3 = \{4, 6\}$

Since $A_1 \cup A_2 \cup A_3 = \Omega$, the events A_1, A_2, A_3 are exhaustive.

Clearly A and A' are exhaustive.

7. Equally likely event : The events A and B of Ω are said to be *equally likely* if chances of occurrence of A and that of be B are equal. In general, events $A_1, A_2, ..., A_n$ are said to be equally likely if chances of occurrence of these events are same.

For example : Consider an experiment of rolling a regular die.

Hence, $\Omega = \{1, 2, 3, 4, 5, 6\}$. Let $A_1 = \{1, 2\}$, $A_2 = \{3, 4\}$, $A_3 = \{1, 6\}$. Since all the sample points have equal chance and of occurrence A_1, A_2, A_3 are equally likely events.

8. Intersection of two events or Simultaneous occurrence of two events : If A and B are the events of Ω then $A \cap B$ is intersection of two events or simultaneous occurrence of two events.

For example : Let $\Omega = \{1, 2, 3, 4, 5, 6\}$

Event A : Occurrence of number multiple of 3

Event B : Occurrence of even number

Clearly $A = \{3, 6\}$, $B = \{2, 4, 6\}$

$\therefore A \cap B = \{6\}$. We say A and B occur simultaneously or $A \cap B$ occurs if outcome 6 occurs.

Similarly, simultaneous occurrence of events A, B, C of Ω is defined as $A \cap B \cap C$.

9. Occurrence of at least one of two events : If A and B are events of Ω then occurrence of at least one of the events A and B is defined as $A \cup B$.

For example : Let $\Omega = \{1, 2, 3, 4, 5, 6, 7, 8\}$

A = Occurrence of even number = $\{2, 4, 6, 8\}$

B = Occurrence of number multiple of 3 = $\{3, 6\}$.

Here occurrence of number either even or multiple of 3 is given by $\{2, 3, 4, 6, 8\}$ which is $A \cup B$.

3.5 Probability of an Event

By probability of an event we mean measure of chance of occurrence of that event. There are various definitions of probability in practice. The simplest one is the classical definition. Classical definition is based on the assumption that all sample points are equally likely i.e. chance of occurrence of any outcome is same. If $\Omega = \{e_1, e_2, ..., e_n\}$ then we assign a number $P(e_i)$ to the sample point e_i which is called as probability of e_i.

If (i) $P(e_i) > 0$ for $i = 1, 2, ..., n$ and

(ii) $P(e_1) + P(e_2) + ... + P(e_n) = 1$.

If the sample points are equally likely or equiprobable then $P(e_1) = P(e_2) = ... P(e_n) = \frac{1}{n}$. Under this situation probability of an event A turns out to be the ratio of number of sample points in set A to the number of sample points in Ω.

Definition : If Ω is a equiprobable sample space and A is an event on Ω then probability of an event A is denoted by $P(A)$ and it is given by,

$$P(A) = \frac{\text{Number of elements in A}}{\text{Number of elements in }\Omega} = \frac{n(A)}{n(\Omega)}$$

or

$$P(A) = \frac{\text{Number of cases favourable to event A (m)}}{\text{Total number of mutually exclusive equally likely and exhaustive cases (n)}} = \frac{m}{n}$$

Illustration 2 : If a pair of unbiased coins is tossed. Obtain probability of occurrence of

(i) both heads.

(ii) single head

(iii) at least one head.

Solution : Here, $\Omega = \{HH, TH, HT, TT\}$

(i) Suppose event A : Occurrence of both heads.

Clearly $A = \{HH\}$, hence $P(A) = \frac{n(A)}{n(\Omega)} = \frac{1}{4}$

(ii) Suppose event B : Occurrence of single head.

Clearly $B = \{HT, TH\}$, hence $P(B) = \frac{n(B)}{n(\Omega)} = \frac{2}{4}$

(iii) Suppose event C = Occurrence of at least one head i.e. occurrence of one or more heads.

Clearly $C = \{HT, TH, HH\}$

Hence, $P(C) = \frac{n(C)}{n(\Omega)} = \frac{3}{4}$

3.6 Important Results on Probability

Result 1 : $P(\phi) = 0$, $P(\Omega) = 1$

Proof : By definition,

$$P(\phi) = \frac{n(\phi)}{n(\Omega)} = \frac{0}{n} = 0 \text{ and } P(\Omega) = \frac{n(\Omega)}{n(\Omega)} = \frac{n}{n} = 1$$

Result 2 : $0 \leq P(A) \leq 1$

Proof : By definition,

$$P(A) = \frac{n(A)}{n(\Omega)}$$

Since, $\quad 0 \leq n(A) \leq n(\Omega)$

We get, $\quad \dfrac{0}{n(\Omega)} \leq \dfrac{n(A)}{n(\Omega)} \leq \dfrac{n(\Omega)}{n(\Omega)}$

i.e. $\quad 0 \leq P(A) \leq 1$

Result 3 : Addition theorem : If A and B are any two events on Ω then

$$P(A \cup B) = P(A) + P(B) - P(A \cap B)$$

Proof : Not included in syllabus.

Corollary : 1. If A and B are mutually exclusive events then

$$P(A \cup B) = P(A) + P(B)$$

Proof : Since A and B are mutually exclusive $A \cap B = \phi$, hence

$$P(A \cap B) = 0$$

Therefore, $\quad P(A \cup B) = P(A) + P(B) - P(A \cap B) = P(A) + P(B)$

Generalization of addition theorem to three events is given below without proof.

Corollary 2 : If A, B, C are any three events on Ω then

$$P(A \cup B \cup C) = P(A) + P(B) + P(C) - P(A \cap B)$$
$$- P(A \cap C) - P(B \cap C) + P(A \cap B \cap C).$$

Result 4 : $\quad P(A') = 1 - P(A)$

Proof : Note that : $\quad \Omega = A \cup A'$, hence

$$P(\Omega) = P(A \cup A')$$

$\therefore \quad 1 = P(A) + P(A') \quad\quad\quad (\because A \cap A' = \phi)$

$\therefore \quad P(A') = 1 - P(A)$

We quote some more results without proof.

Result 5 : If $A \subset B$, then $P(A) \leq P(B)$.

Result 6 : $P(A \cup B) \leq P(A) + P(B)$ (It is called as Boole's inequality)

Result 7 : $P(A \cap B') = P(A) - P(A \cap B)$ and
$P(A' \cap B) = P(B) - P(A \cap B)$

Illustration 4 : If $P(A) = 0.6$, $P(B) = 0.5$, $P(A \cap B) = 0.3$.

Compute $P(A')$, $P(A \cup B)$, $P(A' \cap B)$, $P(A' \cap B')$, $P(A' \cup B')$.

Solution : (i) $\quad P(A') = 1 - P(A) = 1 - 0.6 = 0.4$

(ii) $\quad P(A \cup B) = P(A) + P(B) - P(A \cap B)$
$= 0.6 + 0.5 - 0.3 = 0.8$

(iii) $\quad P(A' \cap B) = P(B) - P(A \cap B) = 0.5 - 0.3 = 0.2$

(iv) Since $(A \cup B)' = A' \cap B'$ (by De Morgan's law)

We get, $\quad P(A' \cap B') = P[(A \cup B')']$
$= 1 - P(A \cup B) = 1 - 0.8 = 0.2$

(v) By De Morgan's law $(A \cap B)' = A' \cup B'$

$P(A' \cup B') = P[(A \cup B)']$
$= 1 - P(A \cap B) = 1 - 0.3 = 0.7$

3.7 Independent Events

Definition : Two events are said to be independent of each other if occurrence or non-occurrence of one does not affect the occurrence or non-occurrence of other event.

Alternatively we can say events A and B are independent if,

$$P(A \cap B) = P(A) \cdot P(B)$$

Result : If A and B are independent events then

(i) A' and B are independent events.

(ii) A and B' are independent events.

(iii) A' and B' are independent events.

Example 1 : In an experiment of tossing a coin,

Event A : Occurrence of head and

Event B : Occurrence of tail.

The events A and B are dependent, which can be verified as follows :

Note that : $\quad P(A) = \frac{1}{2}$, $P(B) = \frac{1}{2}$, $P(A \cap B) = 0$

Hence, $\quad P(A \cap B) \neq P(A) \cdot P(B)$

Therefore, A and B are dependent.

Example 2 : Suppose a card is drawn at random from a well-shuffled pack.

$$\text{Event A} = \text{Getting a spade card}$$
$$\text{Event B} = \text{Getting a king}$$

Clearly, $P(A) = \dfrac{13}{52}$, $P(B) = \dfrac{4}{52}$ and $P(A \cap B) = \dfrac{1}{52}$

Since, $P(A) \cdot P(B) = \dfrac{1}{52}$ we get $P(A \cap B) = P(A) \cdot P(B)$.

Therefore events A and B are independent.

Illustration 5 : If A and B are independent, $P(A) = 0.5$, $P(B) = 0.4$, find $P(A \cup B)$, $P(A' \cap B')$.

Solution : (i) Note that : $P(A \cup B) = P(A) + P(B) - P(A \cap B)$.

Since A and B are independent we get

$$P(A \cap B) = P(A) \cdot P(B)$$

Therefore, $P(A \cup B) = P(A) + P(B) - P(A) \cdot P(B)$

$$= 0.5 + 0.4 - 0.5 \times 0.4 = 0.7$$

(ii) By De Morgan's law we get

$$(A \cup B)' = A' \cap B'$$

∴ $p(A' \cap B') = P[(A \cup B)'] = 1 - P(A \cup B) = 1 - 0.7 = 0.3$

Alternative method : Since A and B are independent, A' and B' are also independent. Therefore,

$$P(A' \cap B') = P(A') \cdot P(B')$$
$$= [1 - P(A)] \times 1 - P(B)]$$
$$= (1 - 0.5) \times (1 - 0.4)$$
$$= 0.5 \times 0.6 = 0.3$$

Solved Examples

Example 3.1 : Two symmetric dice are rolled simultaneously. Find the probability of getting

(i) sum of the numbers on the dice to be 8.

(ii) sum of the numbers on the dice to be even.

(iii) sum of the numbers on the dice to be perfect square.

(iv) sum of the numbers on the dice is either even or perfect square.

(v) numbers on dice are same.

Solution : Since the events are related to the sum, we prepare table showing sum of the numbers on dice for the sake of convenience.

Number on second die	Number on the first die					
	1	2	3	4	5	6
1	2	3	4	5	6	7
2	3	4	5	6	7	8
3	4	5	6	7	8	9
4	5	6	7	8	9	10
5	6	7	8	9	10	11
6	7	8	9	10	11	12

Note that Ω contains $6 \times 6 = 36$ pairs as sample points.

(i) Let, Event A : Sum of the numbers on dice is 8.

∴ $P(A) = \dfrac{m}{n} = \dfrac{5}{36}$

(ii) Let, Event B : Sum of the numbers on dice is even

∴ $P(B) = \dfrac{m}{n} = \dfrac{18}{36} = \dfrac{1}{2}$

(iii) $P\begin{pmatrix}\text{Sum of the numbers on dice}\\ \text{is perfect square}\end{pmatrix} = P\begin{pmatrix}\text{Sum of the}\\ \text{numbers on dice is 4 or 9}\end{pmatrix} = \dfrac{7}{36}$

(iv) $P\begin{pmatrix}\text{Sum of the numbers of dice}\\ \text{is even or perfect square}\end{pmatrix} = \dfrac{22}{36}$

(v) Let, Event C : Getting same numbers on dice
= {(1, 1), (2, 2), (3, 3), (4, 4), (5, 5), (6, 6)}

Hence, $P(C) = \dfrac{6}{36} = \dfrac{1}{6}$

Example 3.2 : A bag contains 6 red and 8 black balls. If two balls are drawn at random one-by-one find probability of getting,

(i) Both the balls of different colour.

(ii) Both the balls of same colour.

Solution : (i) Let Event A = Balls are of different colour.

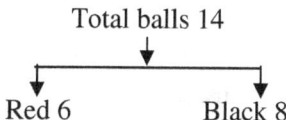

$$\text{Total cases } n = {}^{14}C_2 = \frac{14 \times 13}{1 \times 2} = 91$$

$$\text{Favourable cases} = m = \begin{pmatrix}\text{Number of ways}\\ \text{of getting red ball}\end{pmatrix} \times \begin{pmatrix}\text{Number of ways of}\\ \text{getting black ball}\end{pmatrix}$$

$$= 6 \times 8 = 48$$

$$\therefore \quad P(A) = \frac{48}{91}$$

(ii) If $\quad A$ = Getting balls of different colour.

Clearly $\quad A'$ = Getting balls of same colour

$\therefore$ Required probability = $P(A') = 1 - P(A)$

$$= 1 - \frac{48}{91} = \frac{43}{91}$$

Example 3.3 : Suppose an unbiased coin is tossed 4 times, what is the probability of getting all heads ?

Solution : Let Event A_1 = Getting head in 1st toss

Event A_2 = Getting head in 2nd toss

Event A_3 = Getting head in 3rd toss

Event A_4 = Getting head in 4th toss

P (Getting head at each toss) = $P(A_1 \cap A_2 \cap A_3 \cap A_4) = P(A_1) \cdot P(A_2) \cdot P(A_3) \cdot P(A_4)$

(Since tosses are independent, event A_1, A_2, A_3, A_4 are also independent.

$$= \frac{1}{2} \times \frac{1}{2} \times \frac{1}{2} \times \frac{1}{2} \qquad \left(P(A_i) = \frac{1}{2} \text{ Since coin is unbiased}\right)$$

$$= \frac{1}{16}$$

Exercise 3 (A)

1. Explain the terms with illustrations ?
   (i) Set, (ii) Union of sets, (iii) Intersection of sets, (iv) Complement of a set.
2. Explain the terms with illustration.
   (i) Sample space, (ii) Event, (iii) Independent events, (iv) Mutually exclusive events.
3. Define probability of an event, state the assumptions you make.
4. Write down the sample space of each of the following experiments :
   (i) Examination results of two students are noted.
   (ii) Three coins are tossed simultaneously.
   (iii) Ten radio-sets are checked and number of defective sets are noted.

Exercise 3 (B)

1. If P(A) = 0.6, P(B) = 0.3, P(A ∩ B) = 0.2. Find P(A'), P(A ∪ B), P(A' ∩ B), P(A' ∩ B').

2. Find P(A ∪ B) if P(A) = 0.2, P(B) = 0.5 and given that
   (i) A and B are independent. (ii) A and B are mutually exclusive.

3. If P(A) = 0.6, P(B) = 0.3, P(A ∩ B) = 0.2, find probability that:
   (i) At least one of the two events A and B will happen.
   (ii) exactly one of the two events A and B will happen.

4. A bag contains tickets numbered from 1 to 20. A ticket is drawn at random from the bag. Find the probability that it will bear a number.
   (i) even, (ii) multiple of 3, (iii) even or multiple of 3, (iv) even and multiple of 3.

5. If P(A) = 0.8, P(A ∪ B) = 0.9, P(A ∩ B) = 0.3. Find P(B), P(B'), P(A ∩ B'). Are A and B independent events.

6. If A, B and C are mutually exclusive and exhaustive events on Ω such that:
   P(A) = 2 P(B) = 3 P(C). Find P(A), P(B), P(C), P(A ∪ B), P(A ∪ B ∪ C).

7. Show that, probability of getting 53 Sundays in a leap year is 2/7.

8. A problem in Statistics is given to three students A, B, C whose chances of solving the same are $\frac{1}{2}, \frac{1}{3}, \frac{1}{4}$ respectively. If they solve problem independently. What is the probability that the problem will be solved?

9. Trainee soldiers A, B, C hit target with probability $\frac{1}{3}$ each. If all of them try to hit the target, what is the probability that at least one of them will hit the target?

10. The odds against event A are 5 : 2 and odds in favour of event B are 1 : 1. Find P(A ∪ B) assuming that they are independent.

11. The probability that a contractor will get plumbing contact is $\frac{3}{4}$ and the probability that he will get an electric contract is $\frac{1}{2}$. If the probability of getting at least one contract is $\frac{17}{20}$, find the probability that he will get (i) both the contracts, (ii) exactly one contract, (iii) none of the contracts.

12. A machine has two components A and B. Probabilities that component A and B will fail are 0.2 and 0.15 respectively. What is the probability the machine will fail at any time?

13. Two fair dice are rolled and the sum of the scores is recorded. What is the probability that the sum is
    (i) greater than 4, (ii) less than 8, (iii) 13 or more?

14. A symmetric coin is tossed 4 times. Find the probability that, we will get 2 heads and 2 tails.

15. A peaks the truth in 75% of cases and B in 80% cases. What is the probability that they will (i) say the same thing while stating the fact, (ii) say contradictory things while stating the fact ?
16. An article manufactured by a company consists of two parts A and B. In the manufacturing process of part A, 9 out of 100 are likely to be defective, similarly 5 out of 100 are likely to be defective in the manufacturing of part B. Calculate the probability that the assembled part will not be defective.
17. A husband and wife appear in an interview for two vacancies for the same post. The probability of husband's selection is 1/7 and that of wife's is 1/5. What is the probability that :
    (a) both of them will be selected ?
    (b) only one of them will be selected ?
    (c) none of them will be selected ?

Answers

1. 0.4, 0.7, 0.1, 0.3.
2. (i) 0.6, (ii) 0.7
3. (i) 0.7, (ii) 0.5
4. (i) 0.5, (ii) 0.3, (iii) 0.65, (iv) 0.15.
5. 0.4, 0.6, 0.5.
6. $\frac{2}{5}, \frac{3}{5}$
7. $\frac{3}{5}$
9. $\frac{19}{27}$
10. Odds against event are 5 : 2 means $\frac{P(A')}{P(A)} = \frac{5}{2}$ and odds in favour of event B are 1 : 1 means $\frac{P(B)}{P(B')} = \frac{1}{1}$. Hence, $P(A \cup B) = 9/14$.
11. (i) 2/5, (ii) 9/20, (iii) 3/20.
12. 0.3.
13. (i) $\frac{5}{6}$, (ii) $\frac{7}{12}$, (iii) 0.
14. $\frac{3}{8}$.
15. (i) 0.65, (ii) 0.35.
16. 0.8645.
17. (i) $\frac{1}{35}$, (ii) $\frac{2}{7}$, (iii) $\frac{24}{35}$

Objective Questions

I. Multiple Choice Questions (MCQ) :

1. Suppose $P(A) = 0.7$, $P(B) = 0.8$, if A and B are independent then $P(A \cup B) = $ ......
   (a) 0.94   (b) 0.7   (c) 0.8   (d) 1.5

2. Suppose $P(A) = 0.5$, $P(B) = 0.4$ if A and B are mutually exclusive then $P(A \cup B) = $ ......
   (a) 0.9   (b) 0.7   (c) 0.5   (d) 0.4

3. Suppose $P(A) = 0.5$, $P(B) = 0.4$, $P(A \cap B) = 0.3$, then $P(A' \cap B) = $ ......
   (a) 0.2   (b) 0.1   (c) 0.9   (d) 0.3

4. Suppose $P(A) = 0.5$, $P(B) = 0.4$, $P(A \cap B) = 0.3$, then $P(A \cap B') = $ ......
   (a) 0.2   (b) 0.1   (c) 0.9   (d) 0.3

5. Suppose $P(A) = 0.5$, $P(B) = 0.4$, $P(A \cap B) = 0.3$, then $P(A' \cap B') = $ ......
   (a) 0.7   (b) 0.4   (c) 0.9   (d) 0.2

6. Suppose $P(A) = 0.5$, $P(B) = 0.4$, $P(A \cap B) = 0.3$, then $P(A' \cup B') = $ ......
   (a) 0.7   (b) 0.4   (c) 0.9   (d) 0.2

7. If $P(A) = 5P(A')$ then $P(A) = $ ......
   (a) 5   (b) 1/5   (c) 5/6   (d) 1/6

8. If $P(A) = P(B)$, then
   (a) $A = B$ (b) $A \subset B$ (c) $B \subset A$ (d) none of the above

9. If $P(A \cup B) = P(A) + P(B)$, then ......
   (a) $A \subset B$ (b) $B \subset A$ (c) $A \cap B = \phi$ (d) $A \cap B \neq \phi$

10. If $(A \cup B) = P(A) + P(B)$, then ......
    (a) A and B are mutually exclusive
    (b) A and B are independent
    (c) A is subset of B
    (d) A is superset of B

II. Fill in the Blanks :

11. If $A \subset B$ then $P(A)$ ...... $P(B)$.
12. If $A = \phi$, then $P(A) = $ ......
13. If $A = \Omega$, then $P(A) = $ ......
14. If A and B are mutually exclusive then $P(A \cup B) = $ ......
15. If A and B are independent events then $P(A \cup B) = $ ......
16. $P(A') = 1 - P(......)$
17. $P(A' \cap B) = P(B) - P(......)$
18. $P(A \cap B') = ... - P(A \cap B)$
19. $P(A' \cap B') = 1 - P(...... \cup ......)$
20. $P(A' \cup B') = 1 - P(...... \cap ......)$
21. If A and B are independent then $P(A' \cap B') = $ ......

22. If A and B are independent then $P(A' \cap B) = \ldots\ldots$
23. If A and B are independent then $P(A' \cap B') = \ldots\ldots$
24. If A and B are independent then $P(A \cap B) = \ldots\ldots$

III. State True or False :

25. $P(A)$ is always positive or non-negative.
26. $P(A)$ lies between 0 and 1.
27. $P(A') = 1 - P(A)$.
28. If A and B are any two events of Ω then $P(A \cup B) = P(A) + P(B)$.
29. If A and B are any two events of Ω then $P(A \cap B) = P(A) \cdot P(B)$.
30. If A and B are any two events of Ω then $P(A' \cap B) = P(B) - P(A \cap B)$.

Answers

I. Multiple Choice Questions :
(1) a   (2) a   (3) b   (4) a
(5) b   (6) a   (7) c   (8) d
(9) c   (10) a

II. Fill in the Blanks :
(11) $P(A) \leq P(B)$ (12) $P(A) = 0$ (13) $P(A) = 1$
(14) $P(A \cup B) = P(A) + P(B)$ (15) $P(A \cup B) = P(A) + P(B) - P(A \cap B)$
(16) $P(A') = 1 - P(A)$ (17) $P(A' \cap B) = P(B) - P(A \cap B)$
(18) $P(A \cap B') = P(A) - P(A \cap B)$ (19) $P(A' \cap B') = 1 - P(A \cup B)$
(20) $P(A' \cup B') = 1 - P(A \cap B)$ (21) $P(A' \cap B') = P(A') \cdot P(B')$
(22) $P(A' \cap B) = P(A') \cdot P(B)$ (23) $P(A' \cap B') = P(A') \cdot P(B')$
(24) $P(A \cap B) = P(A) \cdot P(B)$

III. True or False :
(25) True   (26) True   (27) True   (28) False
(29) False   (30) False

Chapter 4...
Binomial Probability Distribution

Contents ...

4.1 Bernoulli Trails

4.2 Binomial Probability Distribution

4.3 Conditions when Binomial Distribution is Used.

4.4 Nature of Graph of p.m.f. of Binomial Distribution

4.5 Mean and Variance of Binomial Distribution

Key Words :

Binomial probability distribution, Bernoulli trials.

Objectives :

To identify the suitable situations for binomial distribution and apply binomial distribution. To find the probability associated with binomial distribution.

4.1 Bernoulli Trials

There are number of experiments having two distinct outcomes. Such experiments are called as **Bernoulli Trials.**

For further study, one of the outcomes of Bernoulli trial is termed as **success** and the other as **failure**. We assign number 1 to success and 0 to failure to define random variable.

Illustrations of Bernoulli trials :

Experiment or Bernoulli trial	Outcomes
(a) Tossing of a coin	Head (1), Tail (0)
(b) Result of a candidate in examination	Success (1), Failure (0)
(c) Sex of a new born baby	Male (1), Female (0)
(d) Item manufactured	Defective (0), Good (1)
(e) State of job in accounts	Completed (1), Not completed (0)
(f) Export consignment	Accepted (1), Rejected (0)

Thus Bernoulli trials can be viewed as a sequence of 0's and 1's. We assign probability p to success or 1 and probability q (q = 1 − p) to failure or 0.

The idea is due to a Swiss mathematician James Bernoulli in 1713, hence it is named as Bernoulli trial.

Suppose Bernoulli trials are repeated n times independently under the identical conditions then the combined result gives binomial probability distribution. For example,

(a) Let X = The number of successful candidates out of n appeared.

The random variable X follows binomial probability distribution.

(b) Let X = The number of machines in working condition out of n machines.

(c) Let X = The number of male births out of n new born babies.

Clearly X gives the number of successes or the number of outcomes of a specific type in n Bernoulli trials. The trials should be :

(i) Identical, i.e. P (success) = p is constant at every trial.

(ii) Independent : i.e. Results of trials are independent.

Thus, there are two parameters of binomial distribution viz. n the number of repetitions of trial and p the probability of success.

4.2 Binomial Probability Distribution

Suppose a trial has two outcomes success (S) with probability p and failure (F) with probability q (q = 1 − p). The result of n trials may be X successes and n − X failures. Thus X is a random variable having binomial probability distribution. Clearly X takes values 0, 1, 2, ... n.

Let us obtain P(X = r). Clearly, the sequence of results have n successes and n − r failures out of n independent trials

$$\underbrace{S, S, S, \ldots S,}_{r} \underbrace{F, F, F, \ldots F,}_{n-r}$$

The corresponding probability will be

$$\underbrace{p, p, \ldots p}_{r} \underbrace{q, q, \ldots q}_{n-r} \quad \text{i.e. } p^r q^{n-r}$$

The r successes can appear in ^nc_r ways.

Thus, $P(X = r) = {}^nc_r \, p^r \, q^{n-r} \quad r = 0, 1, 2, \ldots n; \; 0 < p < 1; \; q = 1 - p$

Meaning of ^nc_r : The number of ways of selection of r objects out of n is denoted by ^nc_r. It is evaluated as follows :

$${}^nc_r = \frac{n!}{r! \, (n-r)!} \quad \text{where } n! = 1 \cdot 2 \cdot 3 \ldots \cdot (n-1) \cdot n.$$

Clearly, $1! = 1$, $2! = 1 \cdot 2 = 2$, $3! = 1 \cdot 2 \cdot 3 = 6$, $4! = 1 \cdot 2 \cdot 3 \cdot 4 = 24$, $5! = 1 \cdot 2 \cdot 3 \cdot 4 \cdot 5 = 120$.

Definition : A discrete random variable X taking values 0, 1, 2, ..., n is said to follow binomial probability distribution with parameters n and p if its probability mass function (p.m.f.) is given by

$$P(X = x) = P(x) = {}^nc_r \, p^x \, q^{n-x} \quad ; \quad x = 0, 1, 2, ..., n$$

$$; \quad 0 < p < 1, q = 1 - p$$

$$= 0 \quad ; \quad \text{otherwise}$$

Notation : Symbolically X follows binomial probability distribution is written as $X \to B(n, p)$. Where n and p are the parameters of the distribution.

Note :

1. The total probability $\sum p(x) = \sum_{x=0}^{n} {}^nc_x \, p^x \, q^{n-x} = (q + p)^n = 1$

2. $P(x) = {}^nc_x \, p^x \, q^{n-x}$ is a general term in the binomial expansion of $(q + p)^n$, hence the probability distribution is called as binomial probability distribution.

3. $Y = n - X$ = The number of failures in n trials. Hence inter-changing the roles of success and failures we get $Y \to B(n, q)$.

4.3 Conditions when Binomial Distribution is used

Binomial distribution is the probability distribution of result of n Bernoulli trials. The trials should satisfy the following conditions :

(a) Every trial should result into the outcomes such as success(S) or failure(F); yes or no; defective or non-defective etc.

(b) The trials should be independent of each other. In other words the outcomes of different trials are mutually independent.

(c) The trials should be conducted under identical conditions. It means probability of success p should be constant at every trial.

(d) The trials should be repeated a fixed number (say n) of times.

Following are some real life examples of binomial random variable.

1. Number of defective items in a lot of n items produced by a machine.
2. Number of male births out of n births in a hospital.
3. Number of correct answers in a multiple choice test of n questions.
4. Number of seeds germinated in a row of n planted seeds.
5. Number of rainy days in a month.

In, all the above situations, 'p', the probability of success is assumed to be constant.

4.4 Graph of p.m.f. of Binomial Distribution of B(n, p)

We plot the values of x on X-axis and p(x) on Y-axis. The histogram appears as follows :

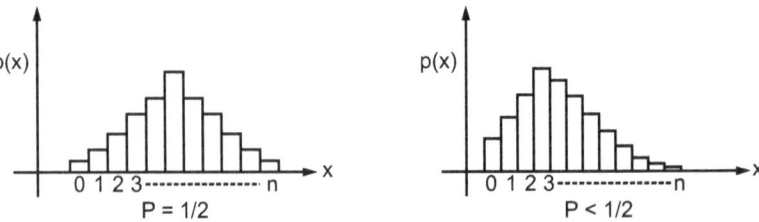

Fig. 4.1 : Symmetric   Fig. 4.2 : Positively Skew

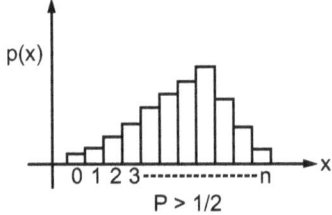

Fig. 4.3 : Negatively Skew

Solved Examples

Example 4.1 : The total daily sell of a departmental store exceeds ₹ 10,000 with probability 1/3. Suppose the store is open on 6 days in week. Find the probability that the sell will exceed ₹ 10,000.

(i) on 4 days, (ii) on atleast 2 days, (iii) on atmost 1 day, (iv) on exactly 2 days, (v) on none of the day, (vi) on all the days.

Solution : Let X be the number of days in week of 6 days with sell more than ₹ 10,000.

Clearly $X \to B\left(n = 6, P = \frac{1}{3}\right)$ and its probability mass function is given by

$$P(X = x) = P(x) = \binom{6}{x}\left(\frac{1}{3}\right)^x \left(\frac{2}{3}\right)^{6-x}, x = 0, 1, 2, \ldots, 6$$

$$= 0 \qquad , \text{otherwise}$$

(i) P (Sell exceeds on 4 days) =

$$P(X = 4) = \binom{6}{4}\left(\frac{1}{3}\right)^4 \left(\frac{2}{3}\right)^2$$

$$= \frac{15 \times 4}{81 \times 9} = \frac{20}{243}$$

(ii) P (Sell exceeds on at least 2 days) = P (Sell exceeds on two or more days)

$$P(X \geq 2) = 1 - P(X < 2) = 1 - P(X = 0) - P(X = 1)$$

$$= 1 - \left(\frac{2}{3}\right)^6 - 6\left(\frac{1}{3}\right)\left(\frac{2}{3}\right)^5$$

$$= 1 - \frac{64}{729} - \frac{192}{729} = \frac{473}{729}$$

(iii) P (Sell exceeds on at most 1 day) = P (Sell exceeds on 1 or less number of days)

$$P(X \leq 1) = P(X = 0) + P(X = 1)$$

$$= \frac{64}{729} + \frac{192}{729} = \frac{256}{729}$$

(iv) P (Sell exceeds on exactly 2 days) = $P(X = 2) = \binom{6}{2}\left(\frac{1}{3}\right)^2 \left(\frac{2}{3}\right)^4 = \frac{80}{243}$

(v) P (Sell exceeds on none of the day) = $P(X = 0) = \binom{6}{0}\left(\frac{1}{3}\right)^0 \left(\frac{2}{3}\right)^6 = \frac{64}{729}$

(vi) P (Sell exceeds on all the days in week) = $P(X = 6) = \binom{6}{6}\left(\frac{1}{3}\right)^6 \left(\frac{2}{3}\right)^0 = \frac{1}{729}$

Example 4.2 : In a quality control department of a rubber tube manufacturing factory, 10 rubber tubes are randomly selected from each day's production for inspection. If, not more than 1 of the 10 tubes is found to be defective, the production lot is approved. Otherwise it is rejected. Find the probability of the rejection of a day's production lot if the true proportion of defectives in the lot is 0.3.

Solution : Suppose X denotes the number of defective tubes in the 10 randomly selected tubes.

∴   X → B (n = 10, p = 0.3)

The production lot is accepted if not more than one tube (i.e. at the most one tube) is found defective.

∴   P (Accepting the lot) = P (X = 0) + P (X = 1)

$$= q^n + npq^{n-1}$$

$$= (0.7)^{10} + 10 \, (0.3) \, (0.7)^9$$

$$= (0.7)^9 \, [3.7] = 0.1493$$

∴   P (Rejection of the lot) = 1 − 0.1493 = 0.8507

4.5 Mean and Variance of Binomial Distribution

$$\text{Mean} = np$$
$$\text{Variance} = npq$$
$$\text{Standard deviation} = \sqrt{npq}$$

Note : Mean > Variance.

Mode :

Case (i) : If $(n + 1) p$ is not integer, then integer part of $(n + 1) p$ is mode.

Case (ii) : If $(n + 1) p$ is integer then there are two modes $(n + 1) p$ and $(n + 1) p - 1$.

Illustration : (a) $X \to B (8, 0.4)$, then find the mean, standard deviation and mode.

Solution :
$$\text{Mean} = np = 8 \times 0.4 = 3.2$$
$$\text{Standard deviation} = \sqrt{npq} = \sqrt{8 \times 0.4 \times 0.6} = \sqrt{1.92} = 1.38$$
$$\text{Mode} = \text{Integer part of } (n + 1) p$$
$$= \text{Integer part of } 3.6 = 3$$

(b) $X \to B (9, 0.4)$, then find the mode.

Solution : Note that : $(n + 1) p = 10 \times 0.4 = 4$ is integer. Hence, here will be two modes 3 and 4.

Example 4.3 : Let $X \to B (n, p)$

(i) Comment on the following : $E(X) = 7$ and $\text{Var}(X) = 12$

(ii) $E(X) = 4$ and s.d. $(X) = \sqrt{3}$. What are the values of n, p and q ?

Solution : (i) $np = 7$, $npq = 12$ $q = \dfrac{12}{7} > 1$ (or $np \geq npq$)

∴ The statement is false.

(ii) $np = 4$, $\sqrt{npq} = \sqrt{3} \Rightarrow npq = 3$

∴ $q = \dfrac{3}{4} \Rightarrow p = \dfrac{1}{4}$ and $n = 16$

Additive Property

Statement : Let $X \to B(n_1, p)$, $Y \to B(n_2, p)$ and X and Y are independent. Then,
$$Z = X + Y \to B(n_1 + n_2, p)$$

Remark : Note that in order to get the above property, 'p' must be the same for both the distributions.

Illustration : Suppose the number of defective items in box A is denoted by X follows $B(n_1 = 10, p = 1/2)$ and the number of defective items in box B denoted by Y follows $B(n_2 = 15, P = 1/2)$. Then the number of defectives in the two boxes combined together is denoted by $X + Y$ and it follows $B(10 + 15, 1/2)$.

∴ $X + Y \to B(25, 1/2)$

Exercise 4 (A) : Numerical Problems

1. If $X \to B\left(8, \dfrac{1}{4}\right)$: find (i) P(X = 3), (ii) P(X < 3), (iii) P(X ≤ 6), (iv) Mean of x, (v) Var (x), (vi) Mode of x.

2. A student prepares for an examination by studying a set of 10 problems. He can solve 7 of the 10. If the professor chooses randomly 5 of the 10 problems for the examination, what is the probability that the student can solve at least 4 of them ?

3. A radar system has a probability of 0.1 of detecting a certain target during a single scan. Find the probability that the target will be detected (a) at least twice in four scans (b) at most once in four scans.

4. If the probability that any person of 65 years old will die within a year is 0.05. Find the probability that out of a group of 7 such persons (i) exactly one, (ii) none, (iii) at least one, (iv) not more than one, (v) all of them will die within a year.

5. Suppose that the probability that a tube light in a class room will be burnt out is 1/3. The class room has in all 5 tube lights and it is unusable if the number of tube lights burning is less than two. What is the probability that the class room is unusable on a random occasion ?

6. A parcel of books contains 10% books with loose binding. What is the probability that a random selection of 6 books will contain 3 books with loose binding ?

7. A real estate agent has 10 houses to sale out in a month. Probability that any house will be sold in month is 0.4. What is the probability that he will sale : (i) only 4 houses, (ii) atleast two houses, (iii) atmost 3 houses (iv) all the houses, (v) none of the house ?

8. In a certain factory there are 20% unskilled workers. In a sample of 10 workers find the probability that :

    (i) exactly 3 will be unskilled.

    (ii) atmost 2 will be unskilled.

    (iii) atleast 2 will be unskilled.

    (iv) none will be unskilled.

    (v) all will be unskilled.

    Also find the average number of unskilled workers and the standard deviation of number of unskilled workers.

9. Suppose $X \to B(5, p)$, $P(X = 1) = \dfrac{5}{32}$, $P(X = 2) = \dfrac{10}{32}$. Find the value of p.

10. Suppose $X \to B(n, p)$.

    (i) If $E(X) = 6$ and $Var(X) = 4.2$, find n and p.

    (ii) If $p = 0.6$, $E(X) = 6$, find n and Var(X).

    (iii) If $n = 25$, $E(X) = 10$, find p and Var(X).

    (iv) Is it possible to have $E(X) = 3$ and $Var(X) = 5$?

Answers

1. (i) 0.2076 (ii) 0.6785 (iii) 0.9996 (iv) 2 (v) 1.5 (vi) 2

2. 0.5282

3. 0.0523, 0.9477

4. 0.2573, 0.6983, 0.3017, 0.9556

5. 0.0453

6. 0.01458

7. (i) $^{10}C_4 \, 0.4^6 \, 0.6^6 = 0.2508$

   (ii) $1 - 0.6^{10} - 4 \times 0.6^9 = 0.8328$

   (iii) $0.6^{10} + 4 \times 0.6^9 + 7.2 \times 0.6^8 + 7.68 \times 0.6^7 = 0.3822$

   (iv) $0.4^{10} = 0.0001$

   (v) $0.6^{10} = 0.0060$

8. (i) $^{10}C_3 \left(\frac{1}{5}\right)^3 \left(\frac{4}{5}\right)^7 = 0.2013$

   (ii) $\left(\frac{4}{5}\right)^{10} + 2\left(\frac{4}{5}\right)^9 + \frac{9}{5}\left(\frac{4}{5}\right)^8 = 0.6778$

   (iii) $1 - \left(\frac{4}{5}\right)^{10} - 2\left(\frac{4}{5}\right)^9 = 0.6242$

   (iv) $\left(\frac{4}{5}\right)^{10} = 0.1074$ (v) $\left(\frac{1}{5}\right)^{10}$

   Mean = 2, S.D. = $\sqrt{1.6}$

9. $\frac{1}{2}$

10. (i) 20, 0.3   (ii) 10, 2.4   (iii) 0.4, 6   (iv) no

Exercise 4 (B)

I. Multiple Choice Questions : Tick mark the correct alternative :

1. If X is binomial random variable then ...
   - (a) mean > variance
   - (b) mean < variance
   - (c) mean = variance
   - (d) mean = standard deviation

2. If X is binomial random variable then the mean and variance are ......
   - (a) np, npq
   - (b) npq, np
   - (c) np, $\sqrt{npq}$
   - (d) $\sqrt{npq}$, np

3. The mode of binomial distribution with parameters n and p when (n + 1) p is not integer is ....
   - (a) np
   - (b) npq
   - (c) integer part of np
   - (d) integer part of (n + 1) p

4. If X → B (10, 0.3) then 10 – X follows binomial distribution with parameters n = ... and p = ...
   - (a) 10, 0.3
   - (b) 10, 0.7
   - (c) 10 – X, 0.3
   - (d) 10 – X, 0.7

5. If X → B (n, p) such that the mean is 18 and S.D. is 3 then the parameters n = ... and p = ...
   - (a) 18, 3
   - (b) 18, 0.3
   - (c) 36, 0.3
   - (d) 36, 0.5

II. Fill in the Blanks :

6. If X → B (10, 0.6), then 10 – X follows ......
7. Binomial distribution is bimodal if (n + 1) p is ....
8. Binomial distribution is symmetric if p is ......
9. The mean and variance of binomial distribution are ...... , ...
10. Sum of 10 Bernoulli trial each having probability of success 0.4 follows ...... distribution.

III. State True or False :

11. Binomial distribution is always symmetric.
12. The variance of binomial distribution is larger than the mean.
13. If X → B (n, 1/2) then n – X → B (n, 1/2).
14. If X → B (n, p) such that the mean is 4 and variance is 3 then n = 16 and p = 0.25.
15. If X → B (10, 1/2), then mode is 6.

Answers 4 (B)

I. MCQ :

1. (a)   2. (a)   3. (d)   4. (b)   5. (d)

II. Fill in the blanks :

6. B (10, 0.4)   7. (n + 1) p is integer   8. p = 1/2   9. np, npq,   10. B (10, 0.4).

III. True or False :

11. False   12. False   13. True   14. True   15. False.

Chapter 5...

Normal Distribution

Contents ...

5.1 Nature of Normal Probability Curve
5.2 Normal Probability Curve and its Properties
5.3 Mean, Mode, Median, Variance of Normal Distribution and Some More Properties
5.4 Computing Normal Probabilities

Key Words :
Normal probability distribution.

Objectives :
To study the nature of normal probability distribution and probability curve. To study the properties of normal distribution. To study the applications of normal distribution.

5.1 Nature of Normal Probability Curve

In the earlier discussion, we have studied how to draw frequency curve. The nature of the curve changes from variable to variable. Some patterns of the curve are given below :

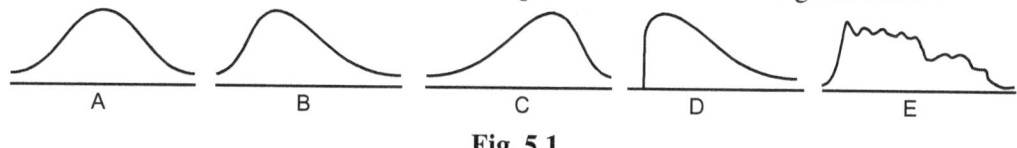

Fig. 5.1

There are many variables such as weight of individuals, height of adult individuals, intelligence quotient of individuals, error in the measurement of length of manufactured item etc. The frequency curve in such cases is like Fig. 5.1. It is bell shaped.

Consider the examples such as income of family, profit of company, electricity consumption, rainfall at a certain place etc. we observe frequency curve like Fig. 5.1 (B) and (C). The score of candidates in competitive examination may resemble a curve of nature given in Fig. 5.1 (D).

If we draw a frequency curve of rise and falls in stock exchange index, we see curve of type 5.1 (E) It has several peaks, hence it is multimodel in nature.

5.2 Normal Probability Curve and its Properties

The curve given by Fig. 5.1 (A) is very commonly observed. Hence, it is called as normal probability curve. The corresponding probability distribution is called as normal distribution of Gaussian distribution.

(5.1)

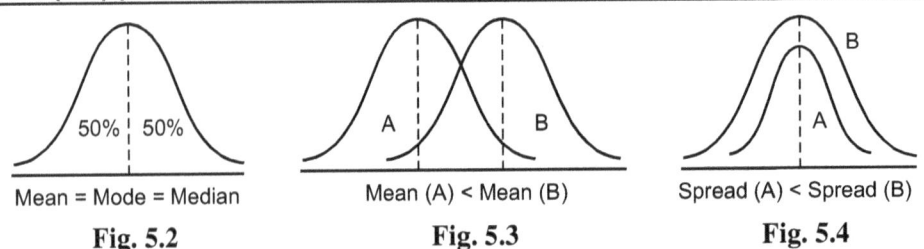

Fig. 5.2   Fig. 5.3   Fig. 5.4

Properties of normal probability curve :

(1) The normal curve is symmetric around the mean. (Fig. 5.2)

(2) It is bell shaped. (Fig. 5.2)

(3) Mean is exactly at the centre. (Fig. 5.2)

(4) Mean divides the curve in two identical parts, hence it is median. (Fig. 5.2)

(5) The curve reaches its peak at mean, hence it is mode. (Fig. 5.2)

(6) Mean, mode, median coincide. (Fig. 5.2)

(7) Curve tapers at both the ends around X-axis but it never meets X-axis.

(8) As mean increases curve shifts to right side (See Fig. 5.3). Similarly, if mean decreases curve shifts to left side.

(9) If the spread of the data is more, curve elongates more on both sides equally (See Fig. 5.4). on the other hand if spread is reduced, the curve will have shorter tails.

(10) Major portion of the curve is around mean. As we go away from mean, height of the curve decreases. The decrease is found to be rapid, if we go further away from mean. Ultimately the height of the curve becomes negligible.

(11) The total area bounded by the normal probability curve and X-axis is considered as 1 unit.

Normal probability distribution is a foundation of further statistical analysis and inference. The curve was discovered by famous mathematician Abraham DeMoivre (1667-1754). The mathematical equation or the formula for the curve was given by Carl Friedrich Gauss (1777-1855). Hence it is called as Gaussian distribution.

Applications of Normal Distribution :

(1) In psychology and educational statistics, intelligence quotient of individuals is considered as normally distributed characteristics.

(2) Marks scored by students in examination are taken to be normally distributed.

(3) In statistical quality control, length, thickness, diameter of parts manufactured are assumed to be normally distributed.

(4) Normal distribution is viewed as limiting distribution or approximation to many probability distributions viz. binomial distribution.

5.3 Mean, Mode, Median, Variance of Normal Distribution and Some More Properties

(1) The mean, mode, median of normal distribution are same and its value is μ.

(2) The variance of normal distribution is σ^2. Thus σ is the standard deviation.

(3) Symbolically we write X follows normal distribution as $X \to N(\mu, \sigma^2)$.

(4) If a random variable X has normal distribution with $\mu = 0$, $\sigma = 1$, the distribution is called as standard normal variable. If is denoted by $N(0, 1)$.

(5) If $X \to N(\mu, \sigma^2)$ then $Z = \dfrac{X - \mu}{\sigma}$ is called as standardized variable. Z follows standard normal probability distribution. Hence, we write $Z = \dfrac{X - \mu}{\sigma} \to N(0, 1)$.

(6) The quartiles of normal distribution are equidistant from μ.

The first quartile $Q_1 = \mu - \dfrac{2}{3}\sigma$

The second quartile $Q_2 = $ Median $= \mu$

The third quartile $Q_3 = \mu + \dfrac{2}{3}\sigma$

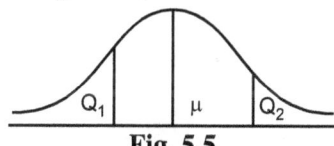

Fig. 5.5

(7) The quartile deviation (Q.D.) of normal distribution

$$= \dfrac{Q_3 - Q_1}{2} = \dfrac{\left(\mu + \dfrac{2}{3}\sigma\right) - \left(\mu - \dfrac{2}{3}\sigma\right)}{2} = \dfrac{2}{3}\sigma$$

(8) The mean deviation (M.D.) of normal distribution about μ is approximately $\dfrac{4}{5}\sigma$.

(9) **The proportion between S.D., Q.D., M.D. :**

Since $\dfrac{M.D.}{S.D.} = \dfrac{\dfrac{4}{5}\sigma}{\sigma} = \dfrac{4}{5} = \dfrac{12}{15}$ ... (1)

and $\dfrac{Q.D.}{M.D.} = \dfrac{\dfrac{2}{3}\sigma}{\dfrac{4}{5}\sigma} = \dfrac{2}{3} \times \dfrac{5}{4} = \dfrac{10}{12}$ ... (2)

We write, Q.D. : M.D. : S.D. : : 10 : 12 : 15
Q.D. is the smallest and S.D. is the longest.
If QD is 10, M.D. will be 12 and S.D. will be 15.

(10) If $X \to N(\mu_1, \sigma_1^2)$, $Y \to N(\mu_2, \sigma_2^2)$, X and Y are independent random variables, then $X + Y \to N(\mu_1 + \mu_2, \sigma_1^2 + \sigma_2^2)$.

5.4 Computing Normal Probabilities

Normal distribution probability is the area under standard normal variable (SNV) curve bounded between the specified ordinates. In general the area table gives area between 0 and ordinate a. We need to use the area between 0 and a to find the area of different events. We discuss below the possible events and their probabilities under SNV. The total area under SNV is = 1.

Area between 0 to ∞ = Area between − ∞ to 0 = 0.5.

Sr. No.	Event	Picture	Probability
1.	$P(Z > 0)$ Positive half of SNV		Area = 0.5
2.	$P(Z < 0)$ Negative half of SNV		Area = 0.5
3.	$P(0 < Z < a), a > 0$		Area between 0 and a
4.	$P(-a < Z < 0)$		Due to symmetry of SNV curve $P(-a < Z < 0) = P(0 < Z < a)$ = Area between 0 and a
5.	$P(Z > a), a > 0$ Area of positive tail		0.5 − Area between 0 and a
6.	$P(Z < -a)$ Area of negative tail		Due to symmetric SNV curve $P(Z > a) = P(Z < -a)$ = 0.5 − Area between 0 and a
7.	$P(a < Z < b)$ Area of strip in positive region		(Area between 0 to b) − (Area between 0 to a)

8.	$P(-b < Z < -a)$ Area of strip in negative region		Due to symmetry of SNV curve $P(a < Z < b) = P(-b < Z < -a)$ = (Area between 0 to b) − (Area between 0 to a)
9.	$P(-a < Z < b)$		Area between (0 to a) + Area between (0 to b)

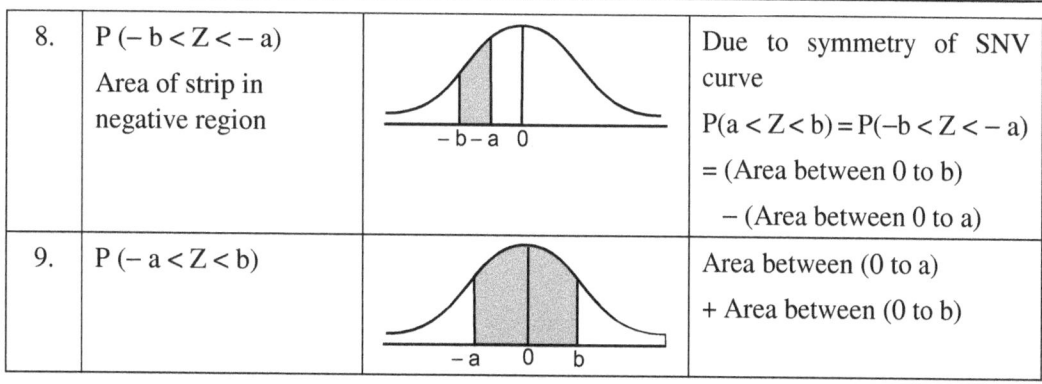

We use the following stepwise procedure to find probabilities related to the events of normal random variable.

(1) Identify the random variable (X) in the given problem.

(2) Identity the values of μ and σ.

(3) Write the event in terms of X. It may be of any type 1 to 9 given in the above table.

(4) Write the event in standard normal variable (SNV). It is nothing but subtract μ and divide the difference by σ. We get

$$P(X > a) = P\left(\frac{X-\mu}{\sigma} > \frac{a-\mu}{\sigma}\right) = P\left(Z > \frac{a-\mu}{\sigma}\right) = P(Z > a') \text{ Z is SNV.}$$

$$P(X < b) = P\left(\frac{X-\mu}{\sigma} < \frac{b-\mu}{\sigma}\right) = P\left(Z < \frac{b-\mu}{\sigma}\right) = P(Z > b')$$

$$P(a < X < b) = P\left(\frac{a-\mu}{\sigma} < \frac{X-\mu}{\sigma} < \frac{b-\mu}{\sigma}\right)$$

$$= P\left(\frac{a-\mu}{\sigma} < Z < \frac{b-\mu}{\sigma}\right) = P(a' < Z < b')$$

(5) We find the required probability using the table value for the specific type described in table.

Solved Examples

Example 5.1 : The weight of sack is normally distributed with mean 50 kg and standard deviation 1.5 kg. Find the probability that the weight of randomly selected sack is more than 51.5 kg. Given that the area under SNV curve between 0 and 1 is 0.3413.

Solution : (1) Suppose X = The weight of sack in kg.

(2) $X \to N(\mu, \sigma^2)$, $\mu = 50$, $\sigma = 1.5$.

(3) Required probability = P (Weight of sack > 51.5)

$$= P(X > 51.5) = P\left(\frac{X-\mu}{\sigma} > \frac{51.5 - 50}{1.5}\right)$$
$$= P(Z > 1) = 0.5 - (\text{Area between 0 and 1})$$
$$= 0.5 - 0.3413 = 0.1586$$

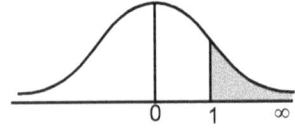

Fig. 5.6

Example 5.2 : An automatic filling machine fills 1 litre of oil in a pauch. The volume of oil filled by machine follows normal distribution with mean 1 litre and the standard deviation is 0.05 litre. The pauch is overfilled if it contains 1.10 litre. Find :

(i) probability that the pauch randomly selected is found to be overfilled.
(ii) percentage of overfilled pauches.

(Gievn that the area under SNV curve between 0 and 2 is 0.47725).

Solution : (i) Suppose X : Volume of oil in a pauch.
(ii) $X \to N(\mu, \sigma^2)$, $\mu = 1$, $\sigma = 0.05$.

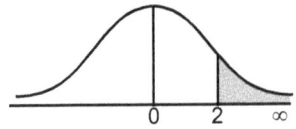

Fig. 5.7

(iii) P (Oil in pauch > 1.10) = P (X > 1.10)
$$= P\left(\frac{X-\mu}{\sigma} > \frac{1.10 - 1.00}{0.05}\right) = P(Z > 2) = 0.5 - (\text{Area between 0 to 2})$$
$$= 0.5 - 0.47725 = 0.02275$$

Percentage of pauches overfilled = P (Oil in pauch > 1.10) × 100
$$= 0.02275 \times 100 = 2.275\%$$

Approximately 2.275% of the pauches will be overfilled.

Example 5.3 : The marks scored by students follow normal distribution with mean 55 and standard deviation 15. Find the percentage of students :

(i) who will pass (if minimum marks for passing is 35).
(ii) who will score 70 and above.
(iii) who will score between 55 and 70.

Given that the area under SNV curve between (i) 0 and 1.333 is 0.3485. (ii) 0 and 1 is 0.3413.

Also state the quartiles.

Solution : Let X = Marks scored in examination, $X \to N(\mu, \sigma^2)$, $\mu = 55$, $\sigma = 15$.

(i) P (Student will pass) $= P(X > 35) = P\left(\dfrac{X-\mu}{\sigma} > \dfrac{35-55}{15}\right) = P\left(Z > -\dfrac{4}{3}\right)$

$= P(Z > -1.3333)$

$=$ Area between $(-1.333$ to $0) + 0.5$

$=$ Area between $(0$ to $1.333) + 0.5$

$= 0.3485 + 0.5 = 0.8485$

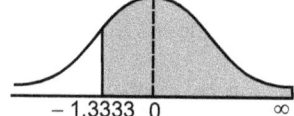

Fig. 5.8

Percentage of passing $=$ P (Student passes) $\times 100\%$

$= 0.8485 \times 100\% = 84.85\%$

(ii) P (Student scores above 70)

$= P(X > 70) = P\left(\dfrac{X-\mu}{\sigma} > \dfrac{70-55}{15}\right) = P(Z > 1)$

$= 0.5 -$ Area between $(0$ to $1) = 0.5 - 0.3413 = 0.1586$

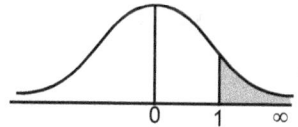

Fig. 5.9

Percentage of students scoring marks above

$= P(X > 70) \times 100\% = 0.1586 \times 100\% = 15.86\%$

(iii) P (Student having marks between 55 and 70)

$= P(55 < X < 70) = P\left(\dfrac{55-55}{15} < \dfrac{X-\mu}{15} < \dfrac{70-55}{15}\right)$

$= P(0 < Z < 1) = 0.3413$

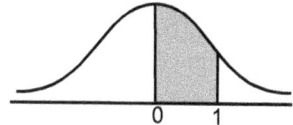

Fig. 5.10

Percentage of students scoring marks between 50 and 70

$= P(55 < X < 70) \times 100 = 0.3413 \times 100 = 34.13\%$

Quartiles : $Q_1 = \mu - \dfrac{2}{3}\sigma = 55 - \dfrac{2}{3} \times 15 = 45$, $Q_2 = 55$, $Q_3 = \mu + \dfrac{2}{3}\sigma = 55 + \dfrac{2}{3} \times 15 = 65$

Example 5.4 : The weight of 1000 students are found to be normally distributed with mean 50 kg and standard deviation 5 kg. Find the number of students with weight :

(i) less than 45 kg.

(ii) more than 60 kg.

(iii) between 45 kg and 60 kg.

(Given that the area under SNV between 0 and 1 is 0.3413 and that between 0 and 2 is 0.4773). **(S.U. Oct. 2010)**

Solution : Let X : The weight of a student, $X \to N(\mu, \sigma^2)$, $\mu = 50$, $\sigma = 5$.

(i) P (Weight is less than 45) $= P(X < 45) = P\left(\dfrac{X-\mu}{\sigma} < \dfrac{45-50}{5}\right) = P(Z < -1)$

$\qquad = P(Z > 1)$

$\qquad = 0.5 -$ Area between 0 and 1

$\qquad = 0.5 - 0.3413 = 0.1586$

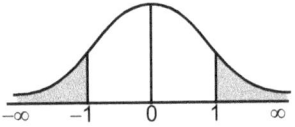

Fig. 5.11

Number of students out of 1000 with weight less than 45

$\qquad = 1000 \times P(X < 45) = 1000 \times 0.1587 = 158.7 \approx 159$

(ii) P (Weight of student > 60) $= P(X > 60) = P\left(\dfrac{X-\mu}{\sigma} > \dfrac{60-55}{5}\right) = P(Z > 1)$

$\qquad = 0.1587$

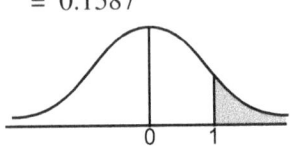

Fig. 5.12

Number of students out of 1000 having weight more than 60

$\qquad = P(X > 70) \times 1000 = 0.1587 \times 1000 = 158.7 \approx 159$.

(iii) P (Weight of student is in between 45 and 60)

$\qquad = P(45 < X < 60) = P\left(\dfrac{45-50}{5} < \dfrac{X-\mu}{6} < \dfrac{60-50}{2}\right)$

$\qquad = P(-1 < Z < 2)$

$\qquad =$ Area between -1 and 0 + Area between 0 and 2

= Area between 0 and 1 + Area between 0 and 2
= 0.3413 + 0.4473 = 0.8186

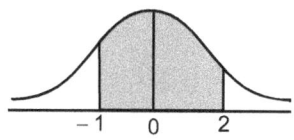

Fig. 5.13

Number of students with weight between 45 and 60 is

= P (45 < X < 60) × 1000 = 0.8186 × 1000 = 818.6 ≈ 819.

Example 5.5 : Let X → N (3, 4). Find (i) P (X > 5) (ii) P (X < 1) (iii) P (X > 0) (iv) P (X < 6) (v) P (2 < X < 6) (vi) P (4 < X < 6) (vii) P (| X | > 4) (viii) quartiles and quartile deviation.

Solution : We need to express first of all the probabilities in terms of standard normal variable Z.

(i) $P(X > 5) = P\left(\dfrac{X - \mu}{\sigma} > \dfrac{5 - 3}{2}\right)$ $(\because \mu = 3, \sigma^2 = 4)$

$= P(Z > 1)$ where, $Z = \dfrac{X - \mu}{\sigma}$

= 0.5 − Area between 0 and 1
= 0.5 − 0.3413 = 0.1587

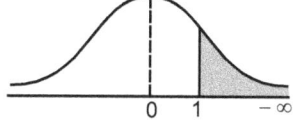

Fig. 5.14

(ii) $P(X < 1) = P\left(\dfrac{X - \mu}{\sigma} < \dfrac{1 - 3}{2}\right)$

= P(Z < − 1)
= P(Z > 1) (due to symmetry)
= 0.5 − Area between 0 and 1
= 0.5 − 0.3413 = 0.1587

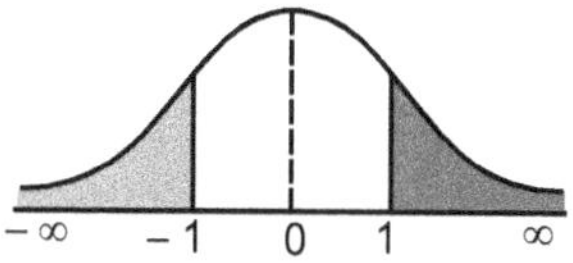

(iii) $P(X > 0) = P\left(\dfrac{X - \mu}{\sigma} < \dfrac{0 - 3}{2}\right)$

= P(Z > − 1.5) = A + B
= Area between 1.5 to 0
= 0.4332 + 0.5 = 0.9332

Fig. 5.15

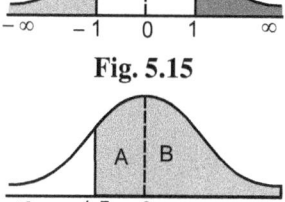

Fig. 5.16

(iv) $P(X < 6) = P\left(\dfrac{X-\mu}{\sigma} < \dfrac{6-3}{2}\right)$

$= P(Z < 1.5) = A + B$

$= 0.5 +$ Area between 0 to 1.5

$= 0.5 + 0.4332 + 0.5 = 0.9332$

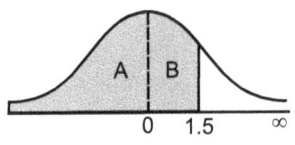

Fig. 5.17

(v) $P(2 < X < 6) = P\left(\dfrac{2-3}{2} < \dfrac{X-\mu}{\sigma} > \dfrac{6-3}{2}\right)$

$= P(-0.5 < Z < 1.5) = A + B$

$=$ Area between 0.5 to 0

$\quad +$ Area between 0 to 1.5

$= 0.1915 + 0.4332 = 0.6247$

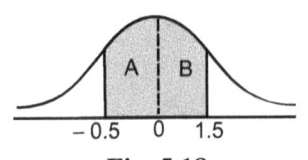

Fig. 5.18

(vi) $P(4 < X < 6) = P\left(\dfrac{4-3}{2} < \dfrac{X-\mu}{\sigma} < \dfrac{6-3}{2}\right)$

$= P(0.5 < Z < 1.5) = A = (A + B) - B$

$=$ (Area between 0 and 1.5) $-$ (Area btween 0 and 0.5)

$= 0.4332 - 0.1915 = 0.2417$

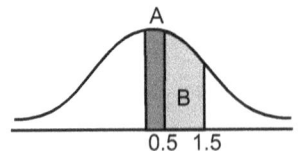

Fig. 5.9

(vii) $P(|X| > 4) = P(X > 4) + P(X < -4)$

$= P\left(\dfrac{X-\mu}{\sigma} > \dfrac{4-3}{2}\right) + P\left(\dfrac{X-\mu}{\sigma} < \dfrac{-4-3}{2}\right)$

$= P(Z > 0.5) + P(Z < -3.5)$

$= [0.5 -$ (Area between 0 and 3.5)$]$

$\quad + [0.5 -$ (Area between 0 and 0.5)$]$

$= [0.5 - 0.4998] + [0.5 - 0.1915]$

$= 0.0002 + 0.3085 = 0.3087$

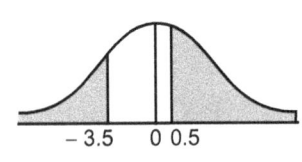

Fig. 5.20

(vii) The first quartile $= Q_1 = \mu - \frac{2}{3}\sigma = 3 - \frac{2}{3} \times 4 = \frac{1}{3}$

The median $= Q_2 = \mu = 3$.

The third quartile $= Q_3 = \mu + \frac{2}{3}\sigma = 3 + \frac{2}{3} \times 4 = \frac{17}{3}$

The quartile deviation $= \frac{Q_3 - Q_1}{2} = \frac{\frac{17}{3} - \frac{1}{3}}{2} = \frac{16}{3 \times 2} = \frac{8}{3}$

Example 5.6 : Suppose heights, of soldiers follow normal distribution with mean 170 cm and variance 49 cm². In a regiment of 1000 soldiers, how many would you expect to be over 184 cm tall ?

Solution : Let X = height of a solider

∴ X → N (170, 49), $\mu = 170$, $\sigma = \sqrt{49} = 7$

Proportion of soldiers having height above 184 cm

$= P(X > 180)$

$= P\left(\frac{X - \mu}{\sigma} > \frac{184 - 170}{\sqrt{49}}\right) = P(Z > 2)$

$= 0.5 -$ Area between 0 to 2

$= 0.5 - 0.4773 = 0.0227$

∴ $\begin{pmatrix} \text{No. of soldiers out} \\ \text{of 1000 having} \\ \text{height above 184 cm} \end{pmatrix} = 1000 \times \begin{pmatrix} \text{Proportion of soldiers} \\ \text{having height above} \\ \text{184 cm} \end{pmatrix}$

$= 1000 \times 0.0227 = 22.7 \approx 23$

Table of area under standard normal variable curve

Ordinates	Area under SNV curve
0 to 0.5	0.1915
0 to 1.0	0.3413
0 to 1.5	0.4332
0 to 2.0	0.4773
0 to 2.5	0.4918
0 to 3.0	0.4987
0 to 3.5	0.4998
0 to ∞	0.5000

Exercise 5 (A)

Theory :
1. State the properties of normal probability curve.
2. State the mean, variance, quartiles, mode and median of normal distribution with parameters μ and σ^2.
3. Sketch the normal probability curve and hence comment why mean = mode = median.
4. State the quartiles of normal distribution. Hence find the quartile deviation.
5. Explain whether normal probability curve is symmetric.
6. What is standard normal variate ? If $X \to N(\mu, \sigma^2)$ how do you find standard normal variate.
7. State the importance of normal distribution in statistical theory.
8. State the uses and applications of normal distribution.
9. State the S.D., Q.D. and M.D. about μ of $N(\mu, \sigma^2)$ hence find the ratio between them.
10. Write a note on normal distribution.

Exercise 5 (B)

Numerical Problems :
1. The life of battery follows normal distribution with mean 300 hours and standard deviation 30 hours. Find :
    (i) Proportion of batteries having life between 270 and 360 hours.
    (ii) Percentage of batteries having life between 270 and 360 hours.
    (iii) Number of batteries out of 500 having life more than 360 hours.
2. Suppose height of an individual follows normal distribution with mean 155 cm and standard deviation 5 cm. If a millitary services appoint an individual with height 160 cm and more. Find the probability that a candidate will be (i) selected, (ii) rejected.
3. A monthly balance on the bank account of a credit card holder is assumed to be normally distributed with mean ₹ 5000 and standard deviation ₹ 1000, find the proportion of credit card holders with balance :
    (i) over ₹ 6500.
    (ii) between ₹ 4000 and ₹ 6000
    (iii) less than ₹ 5000
    (iv) less than the first quartile
    (v) less than the median
    (vi) more than the third quartile.
4. Suppose time taken to complete a certain job in number of days is normally distributed with a mean of 365 days and a standard deviation of 24 days. Find :
    (i) mode, median
    (ii) all the quartiles

(iii) quartile deviation, mean deviation
(iv) the probability that the job will be completed in 401 days
(v) the probability that the job will be completed in 353 days.

5. Suppose life of human being is normally distributed with mean 65 years and standard deviation 8 years. Suppose 100 individuals get a term insurance policy upto age 73 years.
   (i) Find the number of claims out of 100 individuals company is required to pay.
   (ii) If the sum assured is ₹ 1 lac per head, find amount that company has to pay.

6. The rainfall at certain district is normally distributed with 300 cm, with a standard deviation 50 cm. Government decided to give a famine relief fund if the rainfall is below 200 cm. The amount of relief is ₹ 1000 per family. Find the
   (i) probability that a village gets a famine relief fund.
   (ii) average amount the village may get if there are 500 families.

7. A machine manufactures cylinders of diameter with mean 10 cm and standard deviation 0.1 cm. The diameter is normally distributed. If the diameter is more than 10.2 cm it is considered oversize. Find the probability that a cylinder chosen at random is found to be oversize.

8. Electricity consumption in a family is normally distributed with average 180 units and standard deviation 20 units. If the consumption exceeds 230 one has to pay surcharge. Out of 500 families how may have to pay surcharge.

9. The total agricultural production in a year in a certain district is 200 lacks tons with a standard deviation of 50 lacs tons. Find the probability that the agricultural production in a specific year is between 150 lack tons and 275 lacks of tons.

10. Maximum temperature in a heating furnace is normally distributed with 120 centigrade with a standard deviation 5 centigrade. What is the probability that the maximum temperature will
    (i) exceed 127.5 centigrade.
    (ii) lie between 120 and 130 centigrade.

Exercise 5 (C)

I. **Multiple Choice Questions :**
1. If X is normal random variable with mean 50 then $P(X > 50)$ is
   (a) 0 (b) 0.5
   (c) 1
   (d) cannot be obtained since standard deviation is unknown
2. If $X \to N(10, 3^2)$ then the quartiles Q_1 and Q_3 are
   (a) 8, 12 (b) 9.67, 10.33
   (c) 7, 13 (d) 9.25, 10.75
3. If a normal random variable has mean 60 then the mode and median are
   (a) 50, 70 (b) 60, 60
   (c) −60, 60 (d) 0, 60

4. If $X \to N(5, 2^2)$, then …… is a standard normal variate.
   (a) $\dfrac{X-5}{2}$
   (b) $\dfrac{X-5}{4}$
   (c) $\dfrac{X+5}{2}$
   (d) $\dfrac{X-4}{5}$

5. Normal distribution is ……
   (a) symmetric around mean
   (b) positively skew
   (c) negatively skew
   (d) symmetric around 0

II. Fill in the blanks :
6. The normal distribution is symmetric around ……
7. The area under SNV curve between -3 to $+3$ is ……
8. If the mean of $N(\mu, \sigma^2)$ is 5 then median is ……
9. If $X \to N(0, 1)$, then Q.D. is ……
10. If $X \to N(0, 1)$, then M.D. about 0 is ………

III. True or False :
11. Quartiles of normal distribution are equispaced from mean.
12. Normal probability curve is skewed.
13. Standard deviation of normal distribution is smaller than quartile deviation.
14. If $X \to N(5, 3^2)$, $P(X > 5) = P(X < 5) = 0.5$.
15. If $X \to N(0, 1)$, then $P(X < -1) = P(X > 1)$.

Answers 5 (B)

(B) Numerical Problems :
1. (i) 0.8186, (ii) 81.86%, (iii) 409
2. (i) 0.1587, (ii) 0.8413
3. (i) 0.0668, (ii) 0.9546, (iii) 0.5, (iv) 0.25, (v) 0.5, (vi) 0.25
4. (i) 365, 365, (ii) $Q = 349$, $Q_2 = 365$, $Q_3 = 381$, (ii) QD = 16, MD = 19.2 (iv) 0.6915, (v) 0.3085.
5. (i) 0.1587, (ii) 15.87 lacs
6. (i) 0.0227, (ii) $500 \times ₹ 1000 \times P$ (Rainfall < 200) $= ₹ 11,350$.
7. 0.0227
8. 4
9. 0.7745
10. (i) 0.0668, (ii) 0.4773.

Answers 5 (C)

I. Multiple Choice Questions (MCQ) :
1. b 2. a 3. b 4. a 5. a

II. Fill in the blanks :
6. Mean 7. 0.0027 8. 5 9. $\dfrac{2}{3}$ 10. $\dfrac{4}{5}$

III. True or False :
11. True 12. False 13. False 14. True 15. True

Chapter 6...

Time Series

Contents ...

6.1 Introduction

6.2 Meaning of Times Series

6.3 Components of Time Series

6.4 Analysis of Time Series

6.5 Utility of Time Series Analysis

6.6 Measurement of Trend

6.7 Measurement of Seasonal Variations

6.8 Some Real Life Time Series

Key Words :

Time Series, Secular Trend, Seasonal Variations, Cyclical Variations, Irregular Variations, Business Cycles, Additive Model, Multiplicative Model, Moving Average, Least Square Method, Progressive Average, Method of Simple Averages.

Objectives :

Business forecasting needs different models appropriate to the situations. Variables which are time dependent needs different techniques of analysis. Usual techniques used in descriptive statistics are not sufficient. Separation of components in time series and forecasting are two important tasks to be studied in analysis of time series.

6.1 Introduction

In the field of economics, business commerce and management forecasting is often required for several reasons.

Prices of commodities, agricultural production, mineral production, national income, prices of shares, number of passenger travelling from a certain place, revenue collection, population, volume of import and export, volume of foreign exchange, electricity consumption of a city are the examples where the changes take place every now and then. Thus prices, production, consumption are the main areas where the changes are bound to occur with respect to time. In the examples cited, above reliable forecasting needs the knowledge of the reasons behind the changes, the time epochs of changes and the magnitude of changes. The techniques and tools of forecasting are included in this chapter titled 'Time series'. Earlier, we have studied some forecasting tools such as regression lines, fitting of curves, interpolation, etc. However, those tools are useful for longterm, having steady and smooth curve. In reality we rearely see a smooth curve; how to adjust for these temporary fluctuations is studied in this chapter. The examples given above in the field of commerce, economics are called as 'Time series'. The precise definition is discussed subsequently. Number of definitions of time series are available. Some of them are given below.

6.2 Meaning of Time Series

Definition : Time series is a series of statistical observations arranged in chronological order.

The above definition is due to Morris Hamburg. The observations in the chronological order means in the order of occurrence, taken at a regular successive intervals or points of time. The time intervals may be years, months, weeks, days, minutes and seconds also in some cases.

Following are some examples of time series.

1. Daily price of gold.
2. Weekly sales of departmental store.
3. Monthly deposits in a certain bank.
4. Yearly production of food grains in a certain country.
5. Daily record of maximum temperature in a city.
6. Hourly bacterial count in certain culture at laboratory.
7. Population of country at census years.

According to Spiegel, mathematically a time series is defined by the values $Y_1, Y_2, ..., Y_n, ...$ of the variable Y at times $t_1, t_2, ..., t_n, ...$ Thus, time series is a function of time i.e. $Y = F(t)$. In other words, in time series time plays the role of an independent variable and Y (t) is dependent variable. We denote time series by Y (t) or Y_t. In the form of function the time series may be written as follows :

t	t_1	t_2	...	t_n	......
Y_t	Y_1	Y_2	...	Y_n	......

The time points $t_1, t_2, t_3, ...$ are equidistant. The analysis of time series is important from many aspects. We plot t on X-axis and Y_t on Y-axis. Consider, the example of population of India in census years.

Year (t)	1901	1911	1921	1931	1941	1951	1961	1971	1981	1991	2001	2011
Population (Cores) Y_t	23.84	25.21	25.13	27.9	31.87	36.11	43.92	54.82	63.33	84.39	102.70	121.12

We observe that the population is measured during census years with intervals of ten years. Hence, the figures are arranged chronologically, that is in order of time. If they are not ordered according to time, then they would not be able to provide information about the pattern of variation. If you carefully observe the above time series, you will notice that the population has an increasing trend. Now have a look at the following graph.

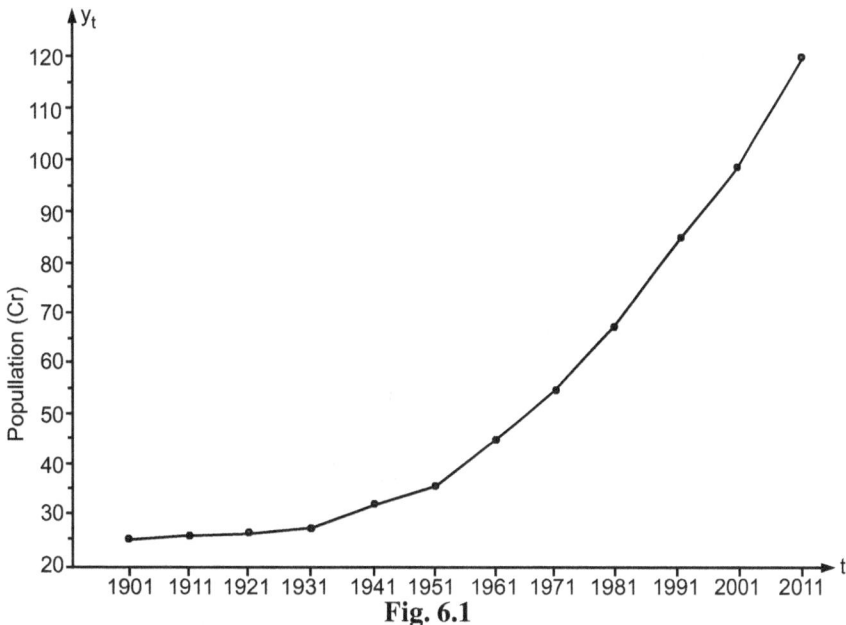

Fig. 6.1

The following things are worth noticing.

(i) India's population is steadily increasing since 1921.

(ii) The rate of population increase accelerates further since 1951, that is, after independence.

Government wants to predict the population of India for future, say for the year 2010; as important policies are to be designed on the basis of such estimates. Time series analysis helps in doing so.

A time series is a summary of past information. Assuming that the 'past' serves a guide to the 'future', time series analysis helps in detecting the underlying patterns and projecting them into future.

Some authors describe the time series data represented graphically as **histogram.**

The nature of time series graph is usually not smooth and not monotonic, it is zig-zag or haphazard. The critical study reveals that these fluctuations are not totally haphazard, however some part is systematic and the only counter part is haphazard in nature.

6.3 Components of Time Series

Time series Y_t is composed of four factors or components viz. (1) Trend, (2) Seasonal variations, (3) Cyclical variations, (4) Irregular variations. These factors cause fluctuations in the values of Y_t. In other words the fluctuations in time series are classified into the above four patterns or categories. A time series may have some or all the components present in it.

1. Trend or Secular Trend (T) :

The trend is the smooth, regular long term movement in time series. It is the general tendency of data. The time series oscillates around trend. The trend may be to go upward to go downword or to remain stagnant.

For example, the yearly population, yearly agricultural production, prices, etc. show an upward trend. On the other hand cost of electronic goods, number of illiterates, yearly birth rates, etc. show downward trend. Yearly rainfall, daily temperature atmospheric pressure at a certain place, monthly electricity consumption of a family are the examples of constant trend. The trend may be linear or non-linear in nature.

Remarks :

(i) Trend is also called as secular trend. The word secular is derived from the Latin word saeculum which means generation or age.

(ii) Trend is due to the reasons of following nature, changes in population, technological developments, changes in economy, changes in habits and tastes of people.

(iii) Trend is a long period movement however, the period cannot be precisely defined. For example, regarding price of gold, agricultural production the long period cannot be few weeks or 2, 3 years. It may be observed over a period of 10 to 15 years even more than that. Long term period may change from series to series.

(iv) Trend is mostly monotonic although original time series is not.

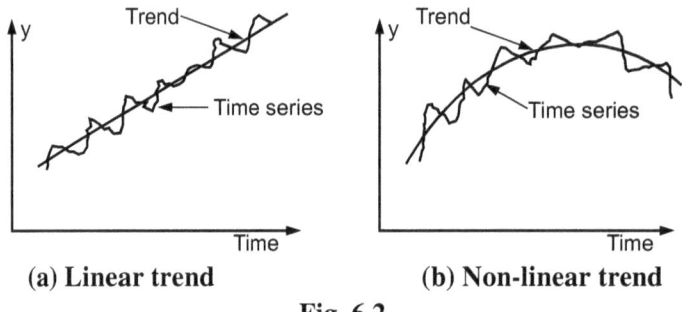

(a) **Linear trend** (b) **Non-linear trend**

Fig. 6.2

In linear trend the values of Y can be approximated by a straight line. This indicates that the rate at 'which the time series values increase or decrease is constant. On the other hand, in non-linear trend, the growth rate is different over different sectors of time. Linear trend is commonly used in business and economics. Non-linear trend is used in the study of population birth rates etc.

(v) Apart from the long-term growth component, there are some short-term periodic rhythmic variations. These variations disturb the smoothness and monotony.

(vi) Trend is useful for two reasons :

   (a) It facilitates the comparison of two time series.

   (b) It helps to extrapolate.

2. Seasonal Variations (s) :

Seasonal variations are the fluctuations in a time series which repeat regularly every year or some specific period of time.

For example, sales of umbrellas and raincoats is the highest in rainy season; sales of wollen garments attains its peak in winter, sales of luxury items and jewellary is high during festivals. Even the bank deposits and bank clearings are affected by seasonal swings. Here, the 'seasons' may be taken as weeks. Similarly, traffic is maximum during rush hours; so 'seasons' are hours in this case. The "seasons' may be seconds in bacterial population growth.

The seasonal variations may be either due to natural forces such as festivals climatic conditions or due to customs, fashions or habits of the people. These factors operate in a regular and periodic manner where the period of recurrence is generally one year. Following graph shows seasonal variations in the sales of umbrellas (Y) from a store.

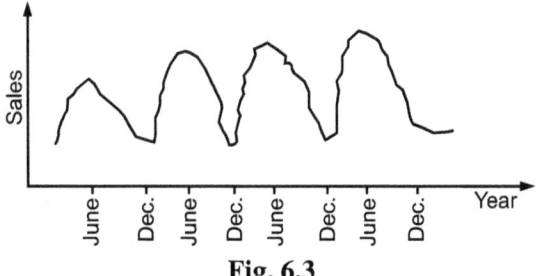

Fig. 6.3

Note that the sales attain maximum in the month of June every year.

Remark : The amplitude may differ from cycle to cycle.

The study of seasonal variations is of prime importance in many time series. Particularly, when the trend is stagnant, seasonal variations become predominant component.

Seasonal variations are extremely useful in marketing and business field in many ways. For example, during summer sales of fans, coolers, refrigerator, cold-drinks, ice-creams increase considerably and reach the peak. Business man has to take care of inventory for seasonal peaks, he has to employ adequate number of salesmen, he has to schedule purchases and sales, he has to arrange for clearance sale, he has to advertise, and give discount on prices for off seasons, he has to arrange for additional finances during seasons. Similarly, bank managers has to arrange for proper cash flow during the beginning of month, festivals.

3. Cyclical variations (c) :

Cyclical variations in a time series are the fluctuations which repeat over a time period of more than one year. The cyclical variations may not be necessarily uniformly periodic. The amplitude of variation also changes from cycle to cycle. That is, the ups and downs may occur at different intervals of time. These fluctuations are typically observed in business. Boom in business is followed by depression and vice-versa. The period of a 'Cycle' is about 7 to 10 years. There are four phases in a cycle. (i) prosperity (boom), (ii) recession, (iii) depression, (iv) recovery. Fig. 6.4 depicts the cyclical variations comprising of these four phases.

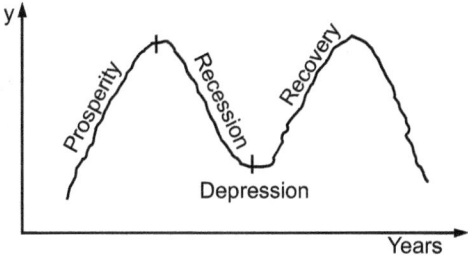

Fig. 6.4

Time series relating to productions, wages bank deposits etc. exhibit cyclical variations in a prominant way.

Business cycle is the main cause behind the cyclical variations. Imbalances in economy, import and export facilities and policies, availability of loans, inflation, over-development, decreasing efficiency of personnel, automation, business competitions are some reasons which result into business cycle.

Difference between 'seasonal variations' and 'cyclical variations' :

(i) Reason : Seasonal variations are evident due to seasons, festivals, customs and needs of people. Whereas cyclical variations exist due to business cycle.

(ii) Period : Seasonal variations are up and down swings of shorter period less than one year. Cyclical variations are of longer period 5 to 10 years or higher in some series. Seasonal variations occur more or less regularly at a certain time period. Cyclical variations may differ in the period from cycle to cycle. They do not occur at a specific period. Both seasonal variations and cyclical variations do not have successive cycles of uniform amplitude.

(iii) Comparatively intensity of seasonal variations less than that of cyclical variation.

4. Irregular Variations (I) :

Irregular variations are unpredictable and are the results of unforeseen forces or abnormal events. These variation therefore do not follow any pattern; neither in their magnitude nor in the time of their occurrence. These variations are generally caused by calamities such as earthquakes, famines floods, epidemics or abnormalities such as war, stikes, lockouts etc. Hence, they are also called as 'episodic fluctuation'.

Irregural variations occur randomly hence they are also called as 'random variations'. These variations are mixed-up with seasonal and cyclical variations. The reasons behind irregular variations are non-recurring hence is difficult to isolate such variations and analyse. Sometimes, the irregular variations are minor in magnitude while in others they are so large due to abnormal reasons, that they produce cyclical variations.

6.4 Analysis of Time Series

Time series analysis, in simple words means, study of time series. The purpose of time series analysis is two fold.

(i) Identifying the above four components which cause variations in the variable, and

(ii) Isolating, studying and measuring each of them independently.

Models for Time Series :

In analysis, it is required to know how the components interact and give the joint effect which is done with the help of models. Generally, two types of models are used to describe a time series Y_t.

1. Additive model :

Let Y denote the original time series and T, S, C, I the four components. Under additive model,

$$Y = T + S + C + I$$

This model assumes that the original time series is mere sum of the four components. In turn, it assumes that the four components have no interaction and act independently. Whenever, the changes are by a constant amount, additive model is used.

Illustration : Suppose a time series has components Trend (T) = 300, Seasonal variation (S) = 90, Cyclical variation (C) = 20 and Irregular component (I) = – 15 at fixed point t then under additive model

$$Y_t = T + S + C + I = 300 + 90 + 20 - 15 = 395$$

The assumption in the additive model is that the components are non-interactive or independent is non-realistic. In order to overcome these limitations, multiplicative model is popularly used.

2. Multiplicative Model :

Under this model, the original time series Y is assumed to be the effect of the four components working interactively. Hence,

$$Y = T \cdot S \cdot C \cdot I$$

In Economics, wherever the changes are by a constant rate, multiplicative model is used.

Using either of these models, the components are eliminated one by one. This elimination helps in isolating the factors from one another and measuring them independently.

There are other types of models also which involve some components additive and some components multiplicative.

For example, $Y = T \times C + S \times I$, $Y = T \times C \times S + I$.

These are beyond the scope of this book.

Illustration : Suppose a time series with multiplicative model has components Trend (T) = 500, Seasonal variation (S) = 1.3, Cyclical variation (C) = 1.2 and Irregular variation (I) = 0.9 at a certain time point t then $Y_t = T \times S \times C \times I = 500 \times 1.3 \times 1.2 \times 0.9 = 702$.

Note :

1. In additive model the components are expressed in terms of actual absolute (not relative) values and Y_t is the algebraic sum of them. However, in multiplicative model the components except trend are interms of relative values or rates or percentage of trend. The trend is expressed in terms of actual value. Y_t in this case is product of all components.

2. Under the additive model the algebraic sum of seasonal variations in a year is zero per year ($\sum S = 0$, per year), that of cyclical variation per cycle is zero ($\sum C = 0$, per year). In the long run sum of irregular variations ($\sum I = 0$).

3. Multiplicative model can be converted to additive if we take logarithms

$$Y = T \cdot S \cdot C \cdot I$$
$$\log Y = \log T + \log S + \log C + \log I$$

6.5 Utility of Time Series Analysis

Time series analysis is of paramount interest in various disciplines such as economics, business, social sciences. Its uses are discussed below :

(i) **Past behaviour :** It enables to describe the past behaviour of the variables. Time series analysis reveals the forces working behind the series such as technological and economical developments, changes in import, export policies.

(ii) **Forecasting :** Forecasting is one of the important use of analysis of time series. The forecasting in business plays important role in planning decision-making, inventory, scheduling of purchases and sales etc.

Isolating and measuring the effects of various components help the investigator to forecast the value of variable in future with fairly good reliability.

(iii) **Comparison :** Time series analysis facilitates the comparison between the two related time series. For example,
   (a) Prices of gold and prices of shares,
   (b) National income and cost of living indices.

Comparison between actual and expected performance can be made comparison between two similar time series at two different places.

6.6 Measurement of Trend

Trend can be estimated by several methods of which we consider the following.

(1) Graphical Method (2) Method of Moving Averages (3) Least squares Method. (4) Method of progressive averages.

(i) **Graphical Method :** This method of estimating trend is also known as "free hand curve fitting" method. It consists of (i) plotting the time series data by taking 'time' on X-axis and the variable of interest on Y-axis and (ii) drawing a smooth free hand curve which would exhibit the long term tendency in the series. [see Fig. 6.5]

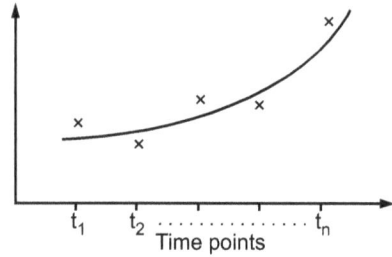

Fig. 6.5

While drawing the curve the following points should be taken care of.
(i) It should be a smooth curve.
(ii) It should pass through as many as points it can.
(iii) Almost equal number of points should lie on either side of the curve. So that the curve is a as close as possible to the points.
(iv) The sum of vertical deviations from the curve should be approximately zero.
(v) Almost equal number of cycles should be on the either side of the curve.

(vi) If the curve bisects the cycles then the area between cycles and curve on both sides should approximately same.
(vii) Fluctuations of smaller magnitude be ignored.

Merits of Graphical Method :
(i) It is the simplest and crudest method of estimating trend.
(ii) It saves time and does not need any mathematical calculations.

Demerits of Graphical Method :
(i) It is rather subjective method. Different persons can get different curves for the same time series.
(ii) Due to this subjectivity, it is dangerous to use this method for forecasting purposes.

(2) Method of Moving Averages : Measurement of trend is possible only when fluctuations arising due to other three components of time series (viz. seasonal, cyclical and irregular) are smoothened out. This is nicely achieved in the method of moving averages. It consists of obtaining arithmetic means of successive overlapping values. The method proceeds as follows.

Suppose the following is a time series.

| Time | t_1 | t_2 | ... | t_n |
| Y | Y_1 | Y_2 | ... | Y_n |

Suppose, we want to find moving averages of period 'm' say. This 'm' called period of moving average is generally taken equal to the time interval for which two successive maxima of y are seen.

The series of moving averages is calculated as follows.

$$\text{First M.A.} = \frac{Y_1 + Y_2 + \ldots + Y_m}{m}$$

$$\text{Second M.A.} = \frac{Y_2 + Y_3 + \ldots + Y_{m+1}}{m}$$

$$\text{Third M.A.} = \frac{Y_3 + Y_4 + \ldots + Y_{m+2}}{m} \text{ and so on.}$$

Two cases arise.

(i) m odd : In this situation moving average is placed against the mid value of the time interval it covers. For example, if m = 5, the moving average will be placed in front of the third value in the group.

(ii) m even : When m is even, the mid value does not coincide with the original time series, in order to make it coincide with the time series, moving averages of order two are again taken. This process is called centering'. (See Ex. 2).

Example 6.1 : The following data give the sales (in '000 ₹) of a company for the years 1985-1994.

Year (t)	1985	1986	1997	1988	1989	1990	1991	1992	1993	1994
Sales (y)	50	82	65	86	70	52	90	65	87	43

Calculate :
(i) 3 yearly moving averages.
(ii) 5 yearly moving averages.
(iii) Plot the original time series alongwith the 3 yearly and 5 yearly moving averages.

Solution :

t	y	3 yearly total	3-yearly m.a.	5-yearly total	5 yearly m.a.
1985	50	–	–	–	–
1986	82	197	65.67	–	–
1987	65	233	77.67	353	70.6
1988	86	221	73.67	355	71.0
1989	70	208	69.33	363	72.6
1990	52	212	70.67	363	72.6
1991	90	207	60.00	264	72.8
1992	65	242	80.67	337	67.4
1993	87	195	65.00	–	–
1994	43	–	–	–	–

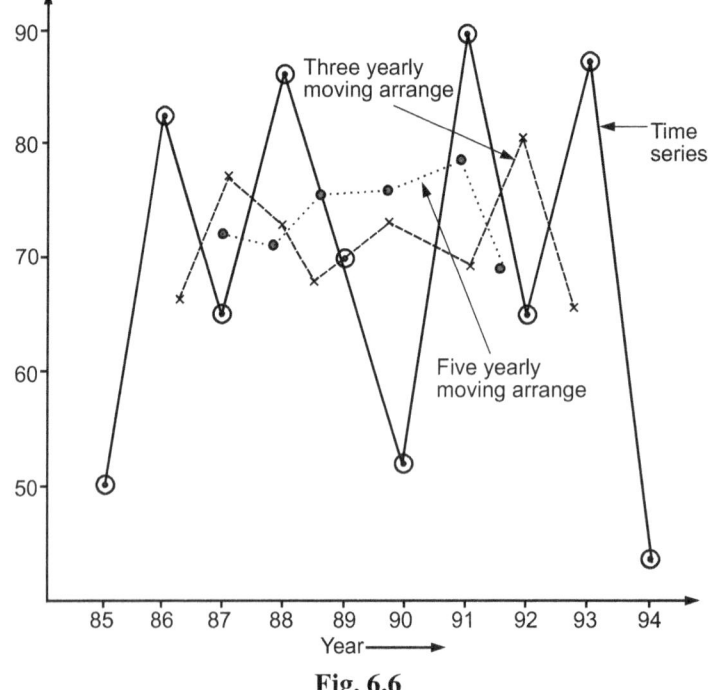

Fig. 6.6

Obtaining Moving Averages using MS-EXCEL

We exhibit how to compute moving averages using MS-EXCEL for the data in example.

Procedural steps :

1. Enter 'years' in column A (Fig. 6.7)
2. Enter 'sales' in column B.
3. Click [Tools] at menu bar. It gives the following window Fig. 6.8.

	A	B	C	D
1				
2				
3	Year	Sales	3-yearly M.A.	5-yealy M.A.
4				
5	1985	50		
6	1986	82	65.6666667	
7	1987	65	77.6666667	
8	1988	86	73.6666667	70.6
9	1989	70	69.3333333	71
10	1990	52	70.6666667	72.6
11	1991	90	69	72.6
12	1992	65	80.6666667	72.8
13	1993	87	65	67.4
14	1994	43		

Fig. 6.7

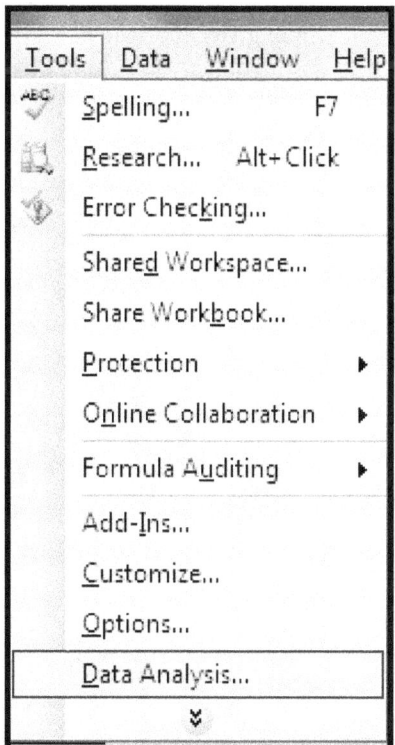

Fig. 6.8

4. Select Data Analysis, which gives Fig. 6.9.

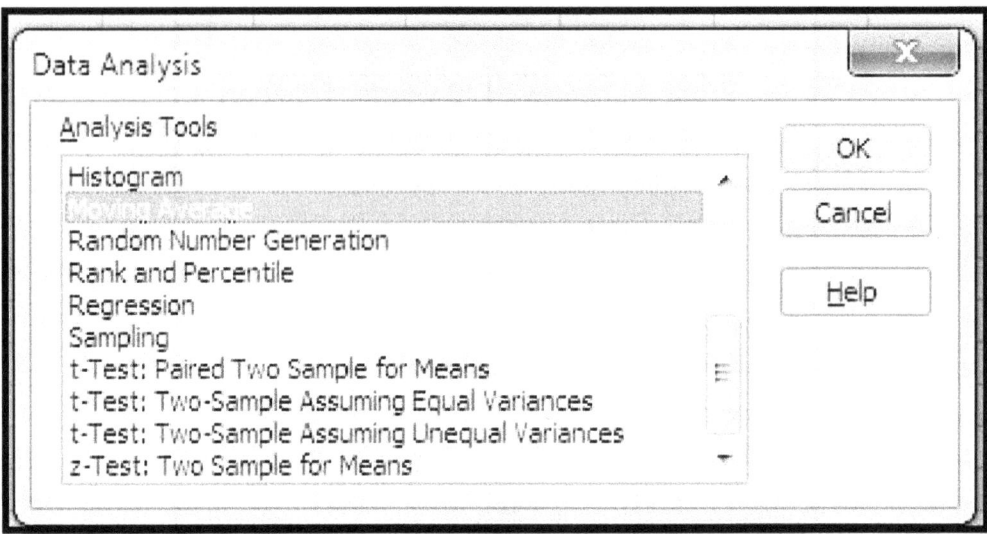

Fig. 6.9

5. Select Moving average, which gives dialogue box Fig. 6.10.

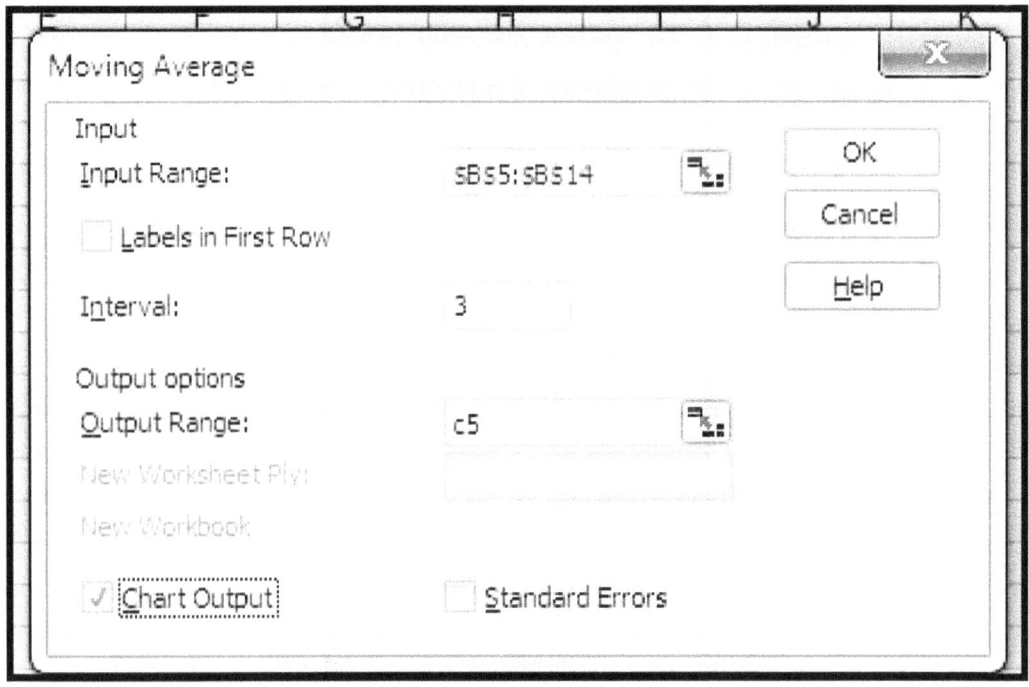

Fig. 6.10

Select input range   B5 : B14

Interval   3   (Period of moving average)

Output range   C5

Select   √ chart output.

It gives graph of original data, moving averages. Fig. 6.11

3-Yearly moving average

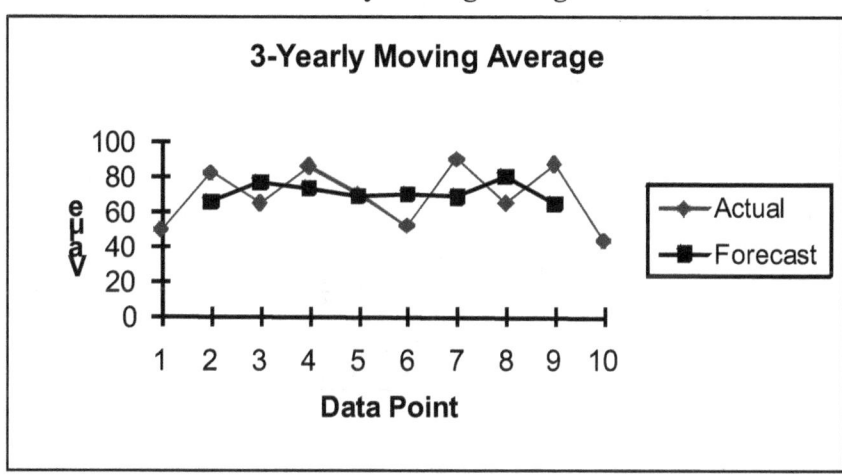

Fig. 6.11

5-Yearly moving average

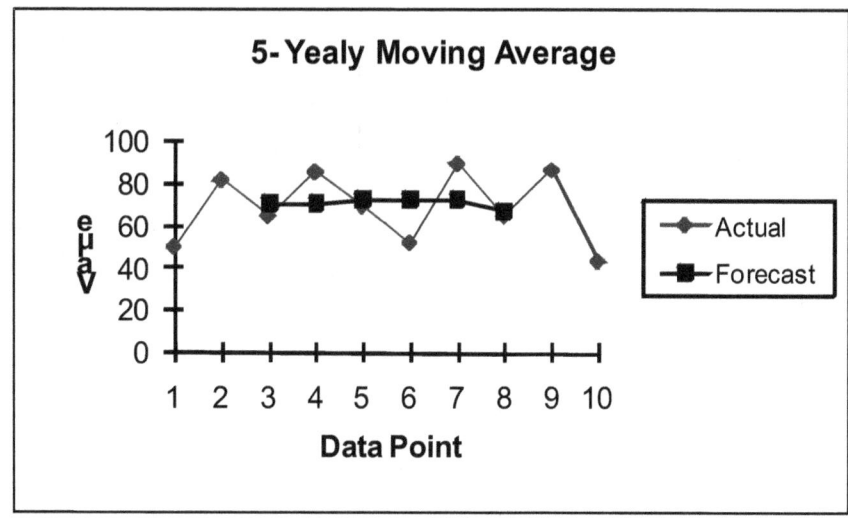

Fig. 6.12

In Fig. 6.7 A column C gives 3-yearly moving averages. Similarly, 5-yearly moving averages can be obtained. Those are shown in column D.

Note : To get moving averages of even order centreing is not done automatically in MS-EXCEL, however we need to take two point moving average.

Example 6.2 : Following data relate to the average retail price ₹ per kg of ground nut during four quarters of 5 years 1998-2002.

Year	Quarters			
	I	II	III	IV
1998	40	35	38	40
1999	42	37	39	38
2000	41	35	38	42
2001	45	36	36	41
2002	44	38	38	42

Obtain 4 point moving average.

Solution : The period of moving average is even, hence it needs to be centred. Thus in the beginning we find 4 point moving average and then 2 point average of these averages. It will ensure centering.

Calculation of moving averages

Year	Quarter	Price Y_t	4-point moving total	4-point moving average	2-point moving total	Centred moving average
1998	I	40				
	II	35				
	III	38	153	38.25	77	38.50
	IV	40	155	38.75	78	39.00
1999	I	42	157	39.25	78.75	39.38
	II	37	158	39.50	78.50	39.25
	III	39	156	39.00	77.75	38.88
	IV	38	155	38.75	77	38.50
2000	I	41	153	38.25	76.25	38.13
	II	35	152	38.00	77	38.50
	III	38	156	39.00	79	39.50
	IV	42	160	40.00	80.25	40.13
2001	I	45	161	40.25	80	40.00
	II	36	159	39.75	79.25	39.63
	III	36	158	39.50	78.75	39.38
	IV	41	157	39.25	79	39.50
2002	I	44	159	39.75	80	40
	II	38	161	40.25	80.75	40.38
	III	38	162	40.50		
	IV	42				

Remark : The 4 point centred moving average is equivalent to a weighted moving average of period 5 with weight 1, 2, 2, 2, 1.

The first centred moving average = 38.50. The five point weighted moving average with weights 1, 2, 2, 2, 1 is

$$\frac{40 + (2 \times 35) + (2 \times 38) + (2 \times 40) + 42}{8} = 38.5$$

Note that first M.A. $= \dfrac{Y_1 + Y_2 + Y_3 + Y_4}{4} = \bar{Y}_1$

Second M.A. $= \dfrac{Y_2 + Y_3 + Y_4 + Y_5}{4} = \bar{Y}_2$

Centred total $= \bar{Y}_1 + \bar{Y}_2$

Centred M.A. $= \dfrac{\bar{Y}_1 + \bar{Y}_2}{2} = \dfrac{1}{2}\left[\dfrac{Y_1 + Y_2 + Y_3 + Y_4}{4} + \dfrac{Y_2 + Y_3 + Y_4 + Y_5}{4}\right]$

$= \dfrac{1}{8} [Y_1 + 2Y_2 + 2Y_3 + 2Y_4 + Y_5]$

= Weighted average of Y_1, Y_2, Y_3, Y_4, Y_5 with weights 1, 2, 2, 2, 1 respectively.

Merits and Demerits of Moving Average Method :

Merits :
(i) The method is simple and easy to work with.
(ii) The method is not subjective.
(iii) A proper choice of period can remove seasonal, cyclical fluctuations completely and irregular fluctuations to some extent.
(iv) The method is flexible in the sense that if few more observations are added to the series, the moving averages obtained earlier remain the same.

Demerits :
(i) The method can not provide trend values for some initial and last points of time.
(ii) It can not be used for forecasting purposes.
(iii) The moving average method estimates the trend fairly well only if the trend is linear, and the ups and downs in the time series are periodic.

(3) Least Squares Method : The method of least square is an analytical method used to estimate the trend values. The relationship between the variable 'Y' and time 't' is assumed according to a mathematical rule.

For example,
(i) $Y = a + bt$ (linear trend)
(ii) $Y = a + bt + ct^2$ (parabolic trend)
(iii) $Y = ab^t$ (exponential trend)
or $\log Y = \log a + t \log b$ (log-linear trend)
(iv) $Y = a_0 + a_1 t + a_2 t^2 + \ldots + a_n t^n$ (n^{th} degree polynomial trend)
(v) $Y = a + bc^t$ (modified exponential trend)
(vi) $Y = ab^{c^t}$ (Gompertz curve)
(vii) $Y = \dfrac{k}{1 + e^{a + bt}}$ (Logistic curve)

How to choose proper type of trend equation ?

The guidelines to choose proper type or trend equation are as follows :

One can use graphical method to get an idea about the nature of curve whether it is straight line or second degree of growth curves such as exponential Gompertz, Logistic curves.

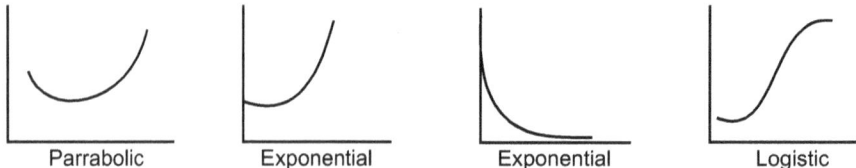

Parrabolic   Exponential   Exponential   Logistic

Fig. 6.13

Note : Modified exponential, Gompertz curve and Logistic curves are called as growth curves. These give best fit for population data or biomass production data.

Once, the curve to be fitted is decided, one can use least square method to fit the curve and estimate constants involved in the equation. The least square method takes care to reduce the sum of squares of errors, where error is the difference between actual value and estimate given by the equation. The method ensures that the points in the data are as close as possible to the curve.

This problem can be looked upon as the problem in regression, where Y is the dependent variable and t, the time, as independent variable. Hence, all the methods of fitting a straight line, fitting a second degree curve or fitting an exponential curve are applicable exactly in the same manner as studied in the earlier year.

Fitting of Linear Trend :

Consider, the model $Y = a + bt$, where a and b are the constants to be estimated. The least squares method obtains the values of a and b such that the sum $\sum (Y - a - bt)^2$ is minimum, where the sum is taken over all pointing the time series. If we change the origin for the variable t and consider $t' = t - \bar{t}$ then the straight line can be written as,

$$Y = a + at'$$

Then the solutions are,

$$\hat{b} = \frac{\sum t' Y}{\sum t'^2}$$

$$\hat{a} = \frac{\sum Y}{n} = \bar{Y}$$

Where, $t' = t - \bar{t}$; $\bar{t} = \frac{\sum t_i}{n}$

Example 6.3 : Fit a trend line to the following time series by the least squares method.

Year (t)	1998	1999	2000	2001	2002
Production (Y) : (in lakh tons)	12	20	28	32	50

Obtain the trend value of production for 2005 and 2007.

Solution : Let the trend line be $Y = a + bt$. Since, $\bar{t} = 2000$, $t' = t - 1998$.

t	y	t'	y'	t'²
1998	12	− 2	− 24	4
1999	20	− 1	− 20	1
2000	28	0	00	0
2001	32	1	32	1
2002	50	2	100	4
Total	142	0	88	10

∴ $\hat{b} = \dfrac{\Sigma t'y}{\Sigma t'^2} = \dfrac{88}{10} = 8.8$

$\hat{b} = \bar{y} = \dfrac{142}{5} = 28.4$

Hence, the trend line is
$Y = 28.4 + 8.8 (t - 2000) = 8.8 t - 17571.6$.
Using this, we estimate y for (i) 2005 and (ii) 2007.
(i) $t = 2005$
then, $y = 28.4 + 8.8 (5) = 72.4$ lakh tons.
(ii) $t = 2007$
     $y = 28.4 + 8.8 (7) = 90$ lakh tons

(4) Progressive Average Method :

Progressive averages are the cumulative average i.e. an average obtained by dividing a cumulative sum by the number of items which makes the sum.

That is, Progressive Average, P.A. = $\dfrac{\sum_{t=1}^{k}}{k}$, k = 1, 2, ...

If the time series values are $y_1, y_2, \ldots$ the progressive average for the first period is y_1, for the second period it is, $\dfrac{y_1 + y_2}{2}$, for the third period it is, $\dfrac{y_1 + y_2 + y_3}{3}$ and so on. Thus to calculate the progressive averages we calculate cumulative sums successfully and divide the sums by 1, 2, 3, ... respectively.

Though it is useful to study the trend during the early stages of an industry and business, it suffers from the defect that, these figures are not suitable as the industry grows up. hence progressive average method should be discontinued as soon as it is not suitable.

Illustration : Calculate the trend values for the following data using progressive average method :

Year	1991	1992	1993	1994	1995	1996	1997
Production (million)	7	10	17	28	43	62	85

Solution :

Year	Production (million)	Progressive Total	Progressive Averages
1991	7	7	7
1992	10	17	8.5
1993	17	34	11.3333333
1994	28	62	12.4
1995	43	105	17.5
1996	62	167	23.8571429
1997	85	252	31.5

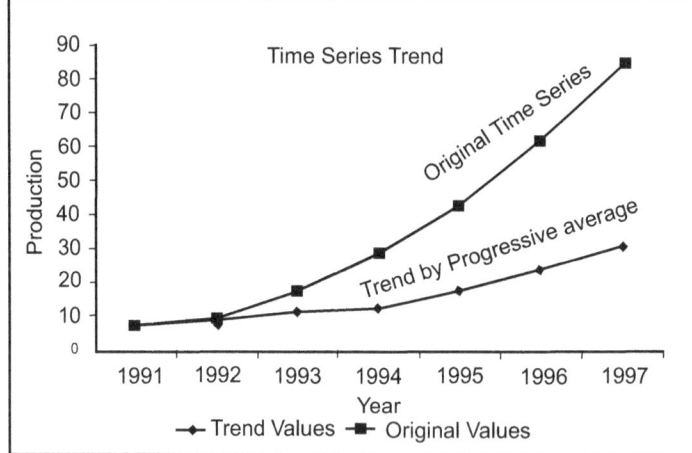

Fig. 6.14

6.7 Measurement of Seasonal Variations

In time series, seasonal variations are those periodic fluctuations which occurs regularly within a period of one year. For instance, demand for cold-drinks in goes up in summer and goes down in winter. During Diwali holidays, there may be increasing demand for sweets and clothes. A business executive has to study the nature of such type of variations in order to take policy decisions regarding inventory, purchase and sale schedule etc.

The important reasons for measurement of seasonal variations are as follows :

(i) To separate the seasonal variation, assuming that those are superimposed on time series. It gives the amount of changes due to seasonal factors in original time series.

(ii) To eliminate the effects of seasonal factors from time series. So that the values in the time series free from seasonal factors can be computed.

The following are different methods of estimating seasonal component of a time series.
(a) Method of simple averages.
(b) Ratio to moving averages method.
(c) Ratio to trend method.
(d) Method of link relatives.

We discuss the simplest method, which is method of simple average.

Method of Simple Averages

It is the simplest method of estimating seasonal variations. The stepwise procedure is as follows :

(i) Arrange the data seasonwise (quarters, months, days) for all the years.
(ii) Compute the totals for each season.
(iii) Compute the arithmetic mean for each season. If there are k seasons then

$\bar{X}_i$ = mean of ith season i = 1, 2, ..., k.

(iv) Compute the mean $\bar{X}$ of seasonal means $\bar{X} = \dfrac{\bar{X}_1 + \bar{X}_2 + ... + \bar{X}_k}{k}$.

In particular, for monthly indices $\bar{X} = \dfrac{\bar{X}_1 + \bar{X}_2 + ... + \bar{X}_{12}}{12}$ where, $\bar{X}_i$ = mean for i^{th} month.

Similarly, for quarterly indices $\bar{X} = \dfrac{\bar{X}_1 + \bar{X}_2 + \bar{X}_3 + \bar{X}_4}{4}$ where, $\bar{X}_i$ = mean for i^{th} quarter.

(v) The seasonal index for i^{th} season = $S_i = \dfrac{\bar{X}_i}{\bar{X}} \times 100$; i = 1, 2, ..., k.

Thus S_i is expressed as percentage of $\bar{X}$.

Remarks : (1) The number of indices is equal to the number of seasons. Thus number of monthly, quarterly and daily indices will be 12, 4, 7 respectively.

(2) The sum of indices is $\sum S_i = 100 \, k$. In particular, sum of monthly indices = 1200, sum of quarterly indices = 400.

(3) Seasonal indices can be obtained by using seasonal totals $(T_1, T_2, ..., T_k)$ instead of seasonal averages as follows :

$S_i = \dfrac{T_i}{\bar{T}} \times 100$ when $\bar{T} = \dfrac{\sum T_i}{k}$

If the data pertains to n years dealy

$S_i = \dfrac{T_i}{\bar{T}} \times 100 = \dfrac{T_i/n}{\bar{T}/n} \times 100 = \dfrac{\bar{X}_i}{\bar{X}} \times 100$.

(4) The indices obtained in this method give rough estimate of seasonal variation due to the reason that the trend is not eliminated. If trend is constant and cycles are absent then the seasonal indices obtained by simple averages will be proper.

Merits :

(1) It is the easiest method.

(2) It is simple to compute seasonal indices by simple averages.

Demerits :

(1) Trend and cyclical variations are not eliminated in this method, assuming that those are insignificant. The assumption is non-realistic.

(2) The seasonal indices by this method gives only rough estimates.

Example 6.4 : Obtain the monthly indices for the following data on production of a commodity by method of simple averages.

Month	Production in lakhs of tonnes in years		
	2010	2011	2012
January	16	19	20
February	15	18	19
March	14	17	18
April	18	20	20
May	19	20	19
June	19	19	21
July	20	21	20
August	17	16	17
September	15	17	14
October	14	16	14
November	16	17	15
December	19	18	19

Solution : We find monthly total for every month.

Let T_i : Total of values for i^{th} month; $i = 1, 2, \ldots 12$

and $\bar{T} = \dfrac{\sum_{i=1}^{12} T_i}{12}$ = Average of monthly totals.

The table given below shows that in this example $\bar{T} = 53$.

Hence, seasonal index for i^{th} month = $\dfrac{T_i}{\bar{T}} \times 100$; $i = 1, 2, \ldots 12$.

Simple averages method for computation of seasonal indices.

Month	Production in lakhs of tonnes			Monthly Total (T_i)	Seasonal index $T_i = \dfrac{T_i}{T} \times 100$
	2010	2011	2012		
(1)	(2)	(3)	(4)	(5)	
January	16	19	20	55	103.7736
February	15	18	19	52	98.1132
March	14	17	18	49	92.4528
April	18	20	20	58	109.4340
May	19	20	19	58	109.4340
June	19	19	21	59	111.3207
July	20	21	20	61	115.0943
August	17	16	17	50	94.3396
September	15	17	14	46	86.7925
October	14	16	14	44	83.0189
November	16	17	15	48	90.5660
December	19	18	19	56	105.6604
Total	–	–	–	636	1200.000
Average	–	–	–	$T = \dfrac{636}{12} = 53$	100

Example 6.5 : The following are the quarterly sales in thousands of rupees for different years. Compute seasonal indices for these data using method of simple averages.

Quarter	Year					
	2007	2008	2009	2010	2011	2012
I	36	36	36	41	42	43
II	40	42	40	47	45	47
III	35	38	38	39	43	44
IV	37	49	41	46	46	48

Solution : Computation of seasonal indices.

Year	Quarters				Total
	I	II	III	IV	
2007	36	40	35	37	–
2008	36	42	38	39	–
2009	36	40	38	41	–
2010	41	47	39	46	–
2011	42	45	43	46	–
2012	43	47	44	48	–
Total (T_i)	234	261	237	267	999
Seasonal index $= \dfrac{T_i}{\bar{T}} \times 100$	93.6937	104.5045	94.8949	106.9069	400

Note :

T_i : Total of ith quarter; i = 1, 2, 3, 4.

$$\bar{T} = \frac{\sum_{i=1}^{4} T_i}{4} = \frac{999}{4} = 249.75$$

∴ Seasonal index for i^{th} quarter $= \dfrac{T_i}{\bar{T}} \times 100$; i = 1, 2, 3, 4.

Example 6.6 : The total sales of a company is expected to be ₹ 60 lakhs during the year, find expected sales in each month given the monthly indices of sales as follows :

Month	Jan.	Feb.	Mar.	April	May	June	July	Aug.	Sept	Oct.	Nov.	Dec.
Seasonal index	110	105	102	101	99	97	92	90	95	100	101	108

Solution : Yearly sales = ₹ 60 lacks.

$$\text{Average monthly sales} = \frac{60}{12} = ₹ 5 \text{ lacks}$$

$$\text{Monthly estimated sales} = \frac{\text{Average monthly sales} \times \text{Seasonal index}}{100}$$

Month (1)	Seasonal index (2)	Estimated sales = $\frac{5 \times \text{col. 2}}{100}$ ₹ in lacks
Jan.	110	5.50
Feb.	105	5.25
Mar.	102	5.10
April	101	5.05
May	99	4.95
June	97	4.85
July	92	4.60
Aug.	90	4.50
Sept.	95	4.75
Oct.	100	5.00
Nov.	101	4.05
Dec.	108	5.40
Total	1200	60.00

6.8 Some Real Life Time Series

The National Sample Survey Office (NSSO) utilizes the data collected by various agencies for the construction of price indices, estimation of poverty, different economic series etc. It helps the centre and state governments in development planning and policy formulation. Thus data analysis of real life time series becomes important. Some illustration are as given below.

(1) Series of index numbers of whole sale prices in India (with base year 2004-2005).

Year	2005-06	2006-07	2007-08	2008-09	2009-10	2010-11	2011-12
Whole sale price Index numbers	108.6	122.6	141.7	145.2	152.9	165.5	170.1

Fig. 6.15 (a) shows increasing linear trend in wholesale price index numbers in India.

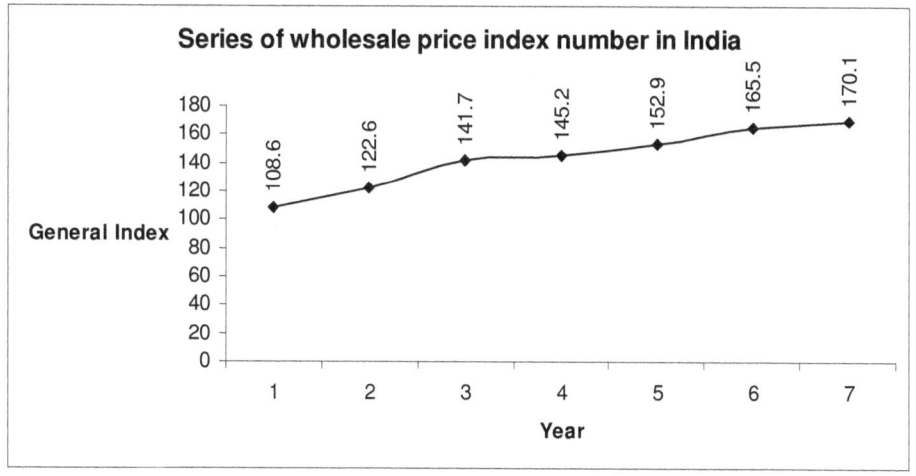

Fig. 6.15 (a)

(2) **Series relating to percentage literacy in India.**

Year	Percentage literacy rate in India	
	Rural	Urban
2003	60	81
2004	61	82
2006	64	83
2007	65	84
2011	69	85

Literacy rate in urban area shows slightly increasing trends while literacy rate in rural area is more increasing trend. However, actual percentage of literacy in rural area is always less than that in urban rural.

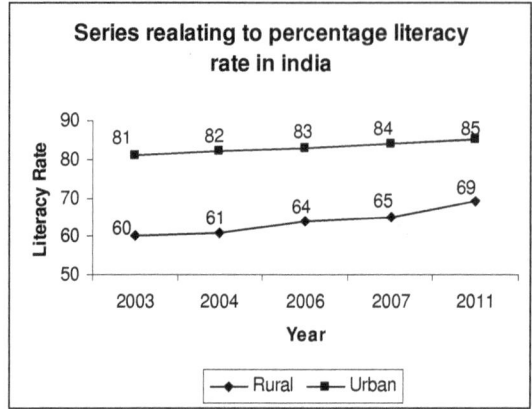

Fig. 6.15 (b)

(3) **Series of gross domestic product (GDP) at facto cost at constant (2004-05) prices in India.**

Year	2004-05	2005-06	2006-07	2007-08	2008-09	2009-10	2010-11
GDP (n ₹ crores) (approximate)	2971000	3542000	3566000	3899000	4158000	4507000	4885000

Fig. 6.16 shows that GDP in India shows strictly increasing trend.

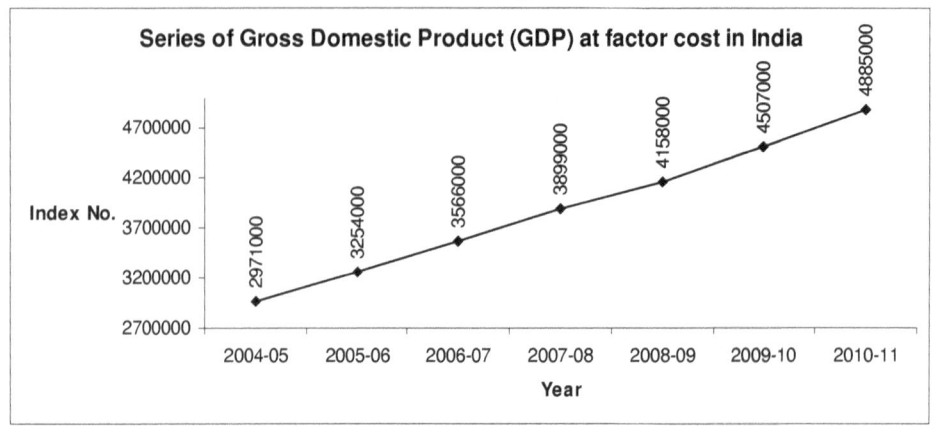

Fig. 6.16

(4) The series of BSE market capital (CAP) in ₹ lakh crores (in India) :

Date	July 2, 2014	July 3, 2014	July 4, 2014	July 5, 2014	July 6, 2014	July 7, 2014	July 8, 2014
BSC Market CAP	91.71	91.56	92.0	92.5	92.1	92.38	89.60

Fig. 6.17 shows no specific pattern in the values of BSE market capital in India.

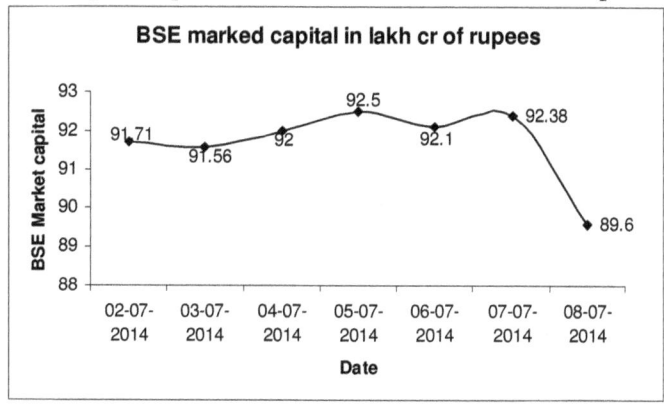

Fig. 6.17

(5) The series of production of natural gas in million cu m (utilized).

Month	March 2013	April 2013	May 2013	June 2013	July 2013	August 2013	September 2013
Production of gas (in million cu m)	3110	2900	2800	2910	2900	2800	2870

Month	October 2013	November 2013	December 2013	January 2014	February 2014
Production of gas (in million cu m)	2810	2980	2960	2910	3000

Fig. 6.18 shows seasonal variation in the production of natural gas in different months in India.

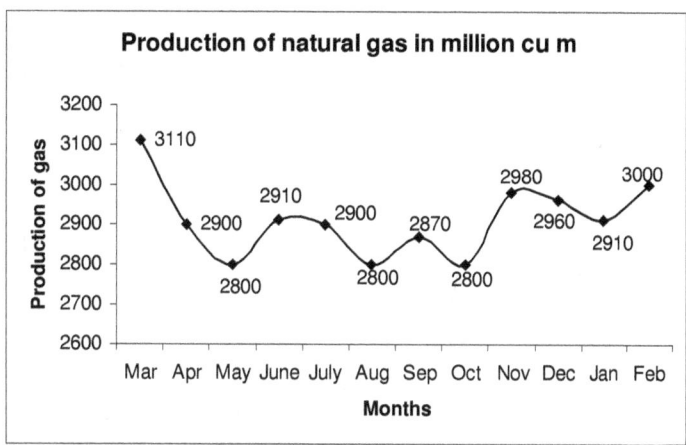

Fig. 6.18

(6) per capita per year income series.

Year	Per capita per year in come (in ₹)
1984	2772
1991	6110
1998	14638
2004	23198
2009	40775
2014	74920

The graph of the per capita per year income series is strictly increasing trend as shown in Fig. 6.19.

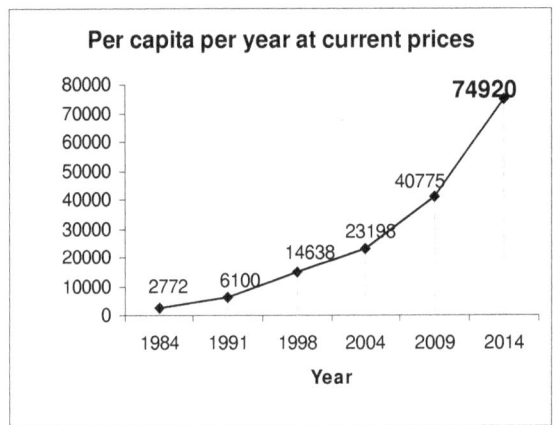

Fig. 6.19

(7) Series of percentage of population below poverty line.

Year	Percentage of population below poverty line
1984	44.5
1991	36
1998	26.1
2004	27.5
2009	27.5
2014	21.9

The graph shows that percentage of population shows decreasing trend from 1984 to 1998 then shows slightly increasing trend during 1998 to 2009 and again shows decreasing trend as shown in Fig. 6.20.

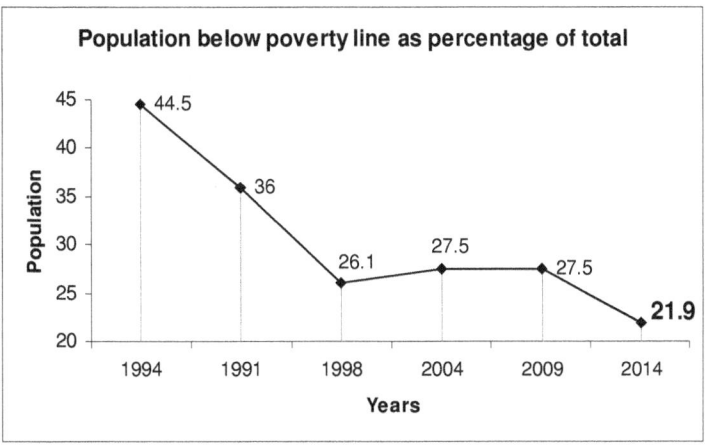

Fig. 6.20

(8) Series of infant morality rates per 1000 live births.

Year	1984	1991	1998	2004	2009	2014
Infant mortality rate per 1000 live birth	104	80	72	58	50	42

Infant mortality rate is also an indicator of health conditions and development of country. The graph 4-28 shows that there is decreasing trend in infant morality in India from 1984 to 2014.

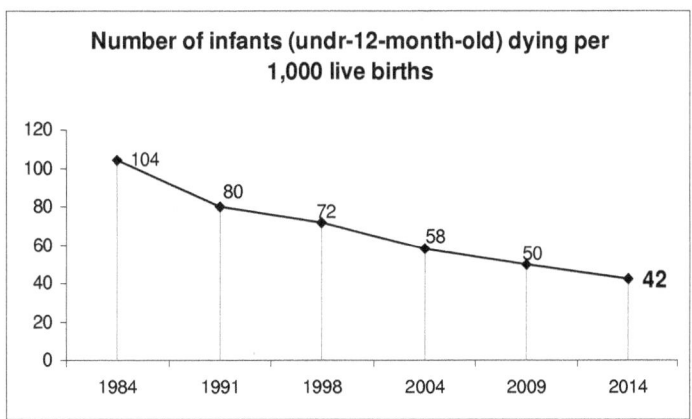

Fig. 6.21

(9) Series of turnover cash market in BSE. (Bombay Stock Exchange)

Date	2/7/14	3/7/14	4/7/14	5/7/14	6/7/14	7/7/14	8/7/14
Turnover in BSE (in crores of ₹ (Approximate))	4300	3400	3800	–	–	4200	4250

Fig. 6.22 shows no specific pattern in the series of turnover in India.

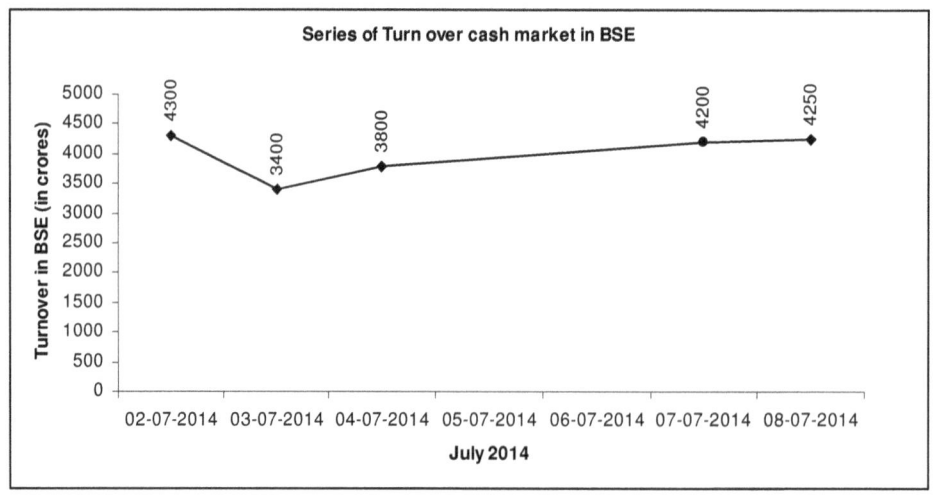

Fig. 6.22

(10) The series of average maximum and minimum monthly temperature in a certain town.

Month	Average maximum temperature (in °C)	Average minimum temperature (in °C)
June 12	8	22
July	26.5	21
August	26	22
September	25.8	20
October	24	19
November	23	15
December 12	22	17
January 13	18	12
February	20	14
March	24	16
April	32	23
May	37	25
June	29	23

July	27	22
August	26	21.5
September	25.2	20.8
October	24	19.5
November	23.5	18
December 13	21	17
January 14	19.5	11
February	21	13.5
March	25	17
April	31	22
May	36	24.5
June 14	27	23

The Fig. 6.23 shows the seasonal fluctuations in maximum and minimum temperatures according to rainy, winter and summer seasons.

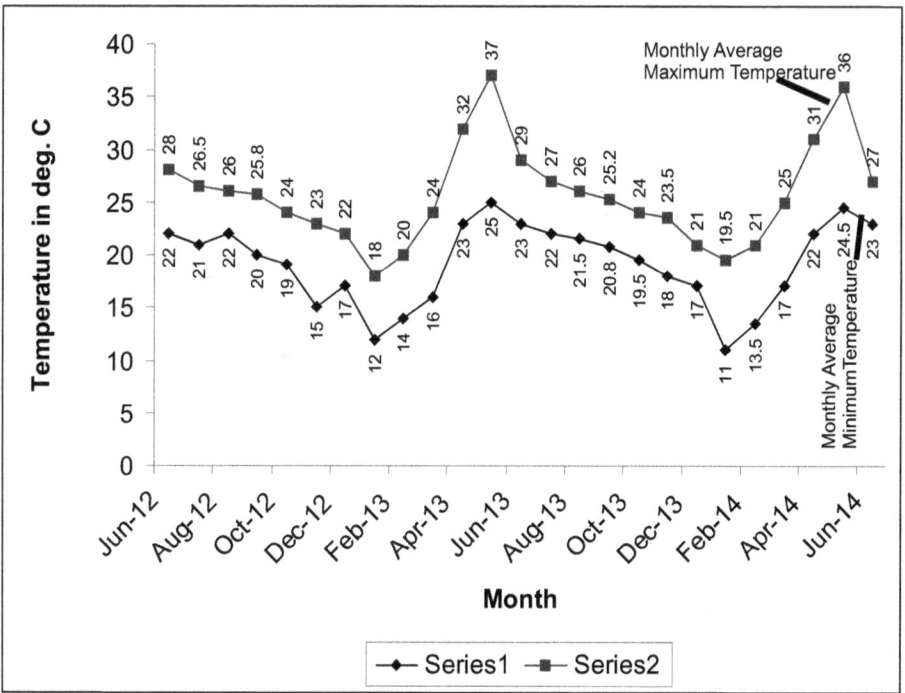

Fig. 6.23

(11) Rain fall (in cm) series over different years in a certain city is as follows :

Year	1995	1996	1997	1998	1999	2000	2001	2002	2003
Rainfall (in cm)	170	178	190	195	150	200	180	185	190

Year	2004	2005	2006	2007	2008	2009	2010	2011	2012	2013
Rain (in cm)	152	205	187	182	192	148	194	176	189	181

The Fig. 6.24 shows that from 1995 generally after 5 years there is less rain fall and in the next year there is more rain fall in the city.

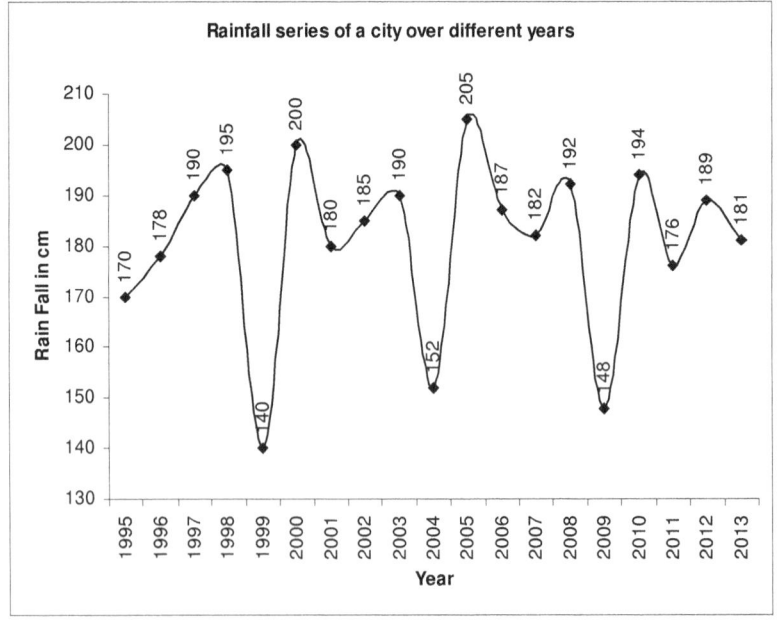

Fig. 6.14

Exercise 6 (A)

(A) Theory Questions :
1. What is a time series ? Give four illustrations of time series in different fields.
2. Define 'time series' and give illustrations of time series from various fields.
3. Discuss the importance and utility of time series analysis in various fields.
4. Discuss the four components of time series.

5. Illustrate with examples the following terms :
   (i) Secular trend.
   (ii) Seasonal variations.
   (iii) Cyclical variations.
   (iv) Irregular variations.
6. Explain in detail the meaning of 'time series analysis'.
7. Discuss long-term and short-term fluctuations in analysis of time series.
8. How would you distinguish the cyclical fluctuations from the trend and the seasonal fluctuations ? Give suitable illustrations.
9. Are all 'periodical movements' necessarily seasonal ? Justify your answer with appropriate illustrations.
10. Explain the different components of a time series with illustrations.
11. What do you mean by 'Secular trend' ? Give two illustrations.
12. Explain the term 'season' used in time series. Also distinguish between seasonal variations and cyclical variations.
13. Explain the concepts of additive and multiplicative models in the analysis of time series. Compare their utility.
14. How do the additive and multiplicative models of the time series differ from each other ? Why is the multiplicative model the most commonly used in time series analysis ?
15. Write a note on irregular variations.
16. Mention the component which is predominant in the following time series. Give explanation of your answer :
    (i) Daily attendance of students in a study hall.
    (ii) Hourly record of the number of customers visiting a restaurant.
    (iii) Prices of shares of a prospering concern.
    (iv) The sales of a departmental store in ₹ over a period of one year.
    (v) Price of residential constructions.
    (vi) Fall in number of deaths as a result of advances in medical science.
    (vii) Reduced production in a factory due to strike.
    (viii) Sales of ice-cream over a period of one year.
17. Describe the term 'Business cycle'. Explain the four phases of business cycle ?
18. Write a note on 'Business Forecasting'.
19. Describe the (i) moving average method and (ii) least square method used for the estimation of trend, (iii) method of progressive averages.

20. Discuss the merits and demerits of (i) moving average method, (ii) least square method used for estimation of trend.

21. Explain how to fit straight line trend, by the method of least square.

22. Explain the following methods of estimating the trend values in a time series.

    (i)   method of moving averages.

    (ii) method of least squares.

    (iii) graphical method.

    (iv) method of progressive averages.

23. Explain the difference between the method of moving averages and method of least squares.

24. Explain when the least square method of estimation of trend is suitable as compared to moving average method.

25. Write notes on (i) business cycle, (ii) seasons in time series.

26. Explain the method of simple averages for obtaining indices of seasonal variations. Discuss its merits, demerits.

27. A power meter went out of order in the month of December, 2014. If the Electric Supply Company has a practice of preparing monthly bills, how should it estimate the power consumption for that month ? The data of power consumption per month are available for the last ten years.

28. State whether each of the following statements is true or false. Justify your answer :

    (i)   Cyclical fluctuations are caused by strikes and lockouts only.

    (ii) An overall tendency of rise or fall in a time series is called as secular trend.

    (iii) If the trend is absent in a time series then seasonal indices are obtained by the method of ratio to trend by moving averages.

    (iv) A seasonal index of 140 for the month of March means that because of seasonal factors the March value will be 40 percent above the monthly average for the year.

    (v)   A need for increased wheat production due to constant increase in population is due to seasonal variations.

29. Write a note on selection of proper method of obtaining trend.

30. State the uses of (i) estimation of trend (ii) estimation of seasonal indices.

31. Explain how to estimate monthly sales given the total yearly sales and seasonal indices for months.

32. Explain when centred moving averages are required to be calculated and why ?

Exercise 6 (B)

(B) Numerical Problems :

1. Estimate trend by using (i) 5 yearly moving average, (ii) 4 yearly centered moving average for the following time series.

Year	Gross Capital Assets (in crores ₹)	Year	Gross Capital Assets (in crores ₹)
1996	19.3	2005	19.3
1997	20.9	2006	18.1
1998	17.8	2007	19.5
1999	16.1	2008	19.2
2000	17.6	2009	22.2
2001	17.8	2010	20.9
2002	18.3	2011	21.5
2003	17.3	2012	21.9
2004	21.4		

2. Estimate trend using 4-yearly centered moving average.

Year	1998	1989	1990	1991	1992	1993	1994	1995	1996	1997
Production (in tonnes)	78	73	71	73	75	78	73	77	70	69

3. Compute 5-yearly moving average and estimate trend.

Year	1	2	3	4	5	6	7	8	9	10	11	12
National Income (in crores)	260	270	275	300	310	315	300	290	310	320	335	380

4. Compute (i) 4-yearly centred moving average (ii) 5-yearly moving average for the following data :

Year	1977	1978	1979	1980	1981	1982	1983	1984
Annual Sales (in lakhs)	3.6	4.3	4.3	3.4	4.4	5.4	3.4	2.4

5. Estimate trend by fitting straight line equation for the following time series.

Year	2009	2010	2011	2012	2013
Sales in 10,000 ₹	35	56	79	80	40

6. Fit a straight line trend to the following data.

Year	2000	2001	2002	2003	2004	2005	2006	2007
Profit in, 000 ₹	90	100	102	93	104	109	102	114

7. The following are the annual profits in thousand ₹ in a certain firm :

Year	2006	2007	2008	2009	2010	2011	2012
Profit	60	72	75	65	80	85	95

By the method of least squares, fit a straight line trend to the above data. Estimate the profit for 2014.

8. Find seasonal indices using method of simple averages for the following time series relating to consumption of monthly electric power in million of KW hours in Maharastra.

Month \ Years	2008	2009	2010	2011	2012
Jan.	40.0	45.0	47.0	50.0	52.5
Feb.	38.0	41.0	43.5	46.0	47.5
March	37.5	39.5	42.5	43.5	50.0
April	34.0	37.0	39.8	41.0	43.5
May	33.0	35.0	37.0	38.0	42.0
June	31.5	33.5	35.0	37.5	39.0
July	32.5	34.0	35.0	38.5	41.5
Aug.	35.0	35.8	38.0	41.0	43.5
Sep.	37.0	38.9	40.0	42.0	46.0
Oct.	40.0	42.0	45.0	46.0	45.0
Nov.	42.0	44.5	47.0	49.0	46.5
Dec.	44.5	46.0	49.0	51.0	49.0

9. Obtain the seasonal indices for the quarters by simple averages method assuming that trend is absent.

Year	Quarters No.			
	I	II	III	IV
2010	37	41	33	35
2011	37	39	36	36
2012	40	41	33	31
2013	33	44	40	40

10. The following data give the sales of a company (in lakhs of ₹) during 1998–2002. Compute seasonal indices by the method of simple averages.

Year	Jan.	Feb.	Mar.	April	May	June	July	Aug.	Sep.	Oct.	Nov.	Dec.
1998	30	40	90	100	80	60	50	60	70	110	100	140
1999	50	60	70	100	100	60	80	70	80	100	110	150
2000	40	70	80	120	90	80	100	60	90	120	110	170
2001	70	50	80	130	110	70	80	80	70	110	110	170
2002	110	130	130	150	170	130	140	80	90	160	220	270

11. Assume that trend is absent, determine the seasonal indices for various quarters given the following data using the simple averages method.

Year / Quarter	2009	2010	2011	2012
Ist	52	57	62	35
IInd	57	48	65	50
IIIrd	54	57	53	54
IVth	58	56	48	52

12. Compute seasonal indices by the method of simple averages using following data :

Year	Cement production (in lakhs of tonnes)			
	Ist quarter	IInd quarter	IIIrd quarter	IVth quarter
2010	8.3	8.1	9.8	11.4
2011	12.4	11.3	11.5	15.2
2012	16.3	16.2	16.8	17.5
2013	19.1	18.0	18.4	16.7

13. Obtain the seasonal indices from the following table by simple averages method.

Year / Quarter	2009	2010	2011	2012	2013
I	400	420	410	450	440
II	350	370	350	360	380
III	380	390	380	360	380
IV	430	310	420	410	420

14. Compute the seasonal indices by the simple averages method.

Year and	2010				2011				2012				2013			
Quarter	I	II	III	IV	I	II	III	IV	I	II	III	IV	I	II	III	IV
Value	75	60	54	59	86	65	63	80	90	72	66	85	10	78	72	93

15. The seasonal indices of sales of garments of a particular type in a departmental store are as follows :

Quarter	I	II	III	IV
Seasonal index	95	87	80	138

If sales in the year is ₹ 20 lakhs estimate quarterly sales.

16. The sale of a company increased from ₹ 50,000 in June to ₹ 58,000 in July. The seasonal indices for June and July are 105 and 140 respectively. The owner of the company is of the opinion that the performance is not upto mark. Justify.

Exercise 6 (B)

5. $y = 58 + 3.4\,(t - 2011)$

6. $y = 101.75 + 1.25 \left(\dfrac{t - 2003.5}{0.5} \right)$

7. $y = 76 + 4.8571\,(t - 2009)$, $\hat{y}_{2014} = 100.2857$.

8. Seasonal indices : 113.2, 104.2, 102.8, 94.3, 89.3, 85.2, 87.6, 93.3, 98.4, 105.2, 110.6, 115.6.

9. Quarterly indices : 98.7, 110.8, 95.3, 95.3.

10. Monthly indices : 60, 70, 90, 120, 110, 80, 90, 70, 80, 120, 130, 180.

11. Quarterly indices : 94.6, 103.04, 102.10, 100.2.

12. Quarterly indices : 106, 96, 94.5, 103.5.

13. Seasonal indices :
    (a) by ratio to moving average : 109.55, 92.77, 98.98, 98.69.
    (b) by ratio to trend : 110.6404, 94.1709, 98.0562, 97.1325.

14. Seasonal indices :
    (a) By ratio to moving average : 122.366, 92.429, 84.694, 100.511.
    (b) By ratio to trend : 121.8127, 92.9702, 83.9948, 101.2223.

15. 4.75, 4.35, 4.00, 6.90 lakhs ₹.

16. Expected sales in July $= \dfrac{\text{Sales in June}}{\text{Seasonal index of June}} \times \dfrac{\text{Seasonal index of July}}{} = \dfrac{50{,}000}{105} \times 140$
    $= ₹\ 66666.67$.

Exercise 6 (C)

I. Fill in the blanks and complete the following statements :

1. In time series values are arranged in .... order.
2. The long term regular movement in a time series is called as ....
3. In time series additive model gives Y = ...
4. In time series multiplicative model gives Y = ...
5. Long term fluctuations in time series is known as .... variations.
6. Short term fluctuations in time series is known as .... variation.
7. Sum of monthly seasonal indices is
    (i) in multiplicative model is ....
    (ii) in additive model is ....

8. Sum of quarterly seasonal indices in
   (i) multiplicative model is …………
   (ii) additive model is …………
9. When the components in time series are inter active ………… model is suitable.
10. When the components in time series are independent ………… model is suitable.
11. If T = 500, S = 90%, C = 80%, I = 120% find the value of time series assuming multiplicative model.
12. If Y = 600, T = 430, S = 90, C = 40 then I = ………… under additive model.
13. Method of moving averages does the important task …………
14. The independent variable in time series is …………
15. The four components in time series are (i) ……… (ii) ………… (iii) ………… (iv) …………..
16. The normal equations to fit trend
    (i) Y = a + bt are …………
17. If Y = a + bt is trend equation then a = $\bar{Y}$ and b = …………
19. Comparison of two time series is possible due to ………… analysis.
19. Daily temperature at certain place is noted as time series. The trend in the time series …………
20. Monthly fluctuations in time series is ………… component of time series.
21. Quarterly fluctuations in time series is ………… component of time series.
22. The effect of strike gives rise ………… component in time series.
23. Periodic changes in time series of period
    (i) less than one year is ………… component.
    (ii) more than one year is ………… component.
24. Ratio to moving average method is used to estimate ………… component.
25. Due to moving averages ………… variations are reduced.
26. The business cycle consists of the following four stages (i) ………… (ii) ………… (iii) ………… (iv) …………
27. The moving averages of ………… period needs to be centred.
28. If the trend equation is Y = a + bt then b is invariant under the change of …………
29. Increased sales due to Diwali is due to ………… component in time series.
30. General decline in cotton cloth sales is ………… component in time series.

31. Increasing population is .... component of time series.
32. Increase in prices of food grains due to famine, of flood constitutes .... component of time series.

II. Multiple Choice Questions :

Choose the correct alternatives Q. 35 to Q. 44.

33. Secular trend in time series is of nature
    (a) increasing (b) decreasing (c) stagnant (d) all the above.
34. Linear trend means
    (a) no change (b) constant change (c) changes are in geometric progression
    (d) none of the above.
35. Moving averages remove the cyclical variation if
    (a) the period is even
    (b) the period is odd
    (c) the average is weighted
    (d) the period is same as that of cycle.
36. Moving average method is not suitable for
    (a) removing rhythmic variations
    (b) projections
    (c) estimating seasonal variations
    (d) none of the above
37. Moving average methods suffers from the drawback.
    (a) It is a subjective method.
    (b) It does not estimate trend for all the time points.
    (c) both (a) and (b) are true
    (d) neither (a) nor (b) is time
38. Least square method
    (a) reduces the calculations.
    (b) does not give estimate for future.
    (c) reduces the sum of squares of errors.
    (d) is subjective.
39. In time series analysis the method of moving averages, is used to estimate
    (a) seasonal variations   (b) trend
    (c) cyclical variations   (d) irregular variations
40. In time series analysis, method of simple averages is used to estimate
    (a) trend   (b) seasonal variations
    (c) cyclical variations   (d) irregular variations

III. State True or False :

41. Trend is the long term movement in time series.
42. Seasonal variations have period less than one year. **(Oct. 2009)**
43. The observations in time series are independent of each other.
44. Irregular variations are predictable in the analysis of time series.
45. The sum of quarterly seasonal indices is 400, if the model is multiplicative.
46. Moving averages can give estimate of trend for future.
47. Autoregressive model is a special case of additive model.
48. If trend is absent simple averages give proper estimates of seaonal indices.
49. Seasonal variations depend upon business cycle.
50. Seasonal variations are short term variations.

Answers 6 (C)

I. 1. chronological
    2. trend
    3. $Y = T + S + C + I$
    4. $Y = T \cdot S \cdot C \cdot I$
    5. cyclical
    6. seasonal
    7. (i) 1200
    7. (ii) 0
    8. (i) 400
    8. (ii) 0
    9. multiplicative
    10. additive
    11. 432
    12. 50
    13. removes rhythmic fluctuations
    14. time
    15. trend, seasonal variation, cyclical variation, irregular variation.
    16. (i) $\sum y = na + b \sum t$
        $\sum y_t = a \sum b + b \sum t^2$
    17. $\dfrac{\frac{1}{n} \sum yt - \bar{y} \cdot \bar{t}}{\frac{\sum t^2}{n} - \bar{t}^2}$
    18. time series
    19. constant
    20. seasonal
    21. seasonal
    22. irregular
    23. (i) seasonal (ii) cyclical
    24. seasonal
    25. cyclical

26. prosperity, recession, depression, recovery
27. even
28. origin
29. seasonal
30. trend
31. trend
32. irregular

II. 33. (d)
34. (b)
35. (d)
36. (b)
37. (b)
38. (c).
39. (b)
40. (b)

III. 41. True
42. True
43. False
44. False
45. True
46. False
47. False
48. True
49. False
50. True

□□□

Time : 2 Hours]   **Specimen Question Paper**   [Maximum Marks : 50

Instructions :
1. All questions are compulsory.
2. Figures to the **right** indicate **full** marks.
3. Use of calculator is allowed.
5. Graph papers will be supplied on request.

1. **Choose the correct alternative :** (1 × 10)

   (A) The control limits for R chart when standards are not given are ......

   (a) $A_2\bar{R}$ (b) $D_3\bar{R}, D_4\bar{R}$

   (c) $D_1\bar{R}, D_2\bar{R}$ (d) $d_3\bar{R}, d_4\bar{R}$

   (B) P chart is appropriate when the characteristics is ......

   (a) variable (b) attribute

   (c) discrete variable (d) continuous variable

   (C) The purpose of price index number is to ......

   (a) forecast prices in future

   (b) find the average increase in the prices of commodities

   (c) find the average decrease in the price of commodities

   (d) find the average change price of commodities

   (D) If Laspeyre's price index number is 121, Paasche's price index number is 100 then the Fishers's price index number is ......

   (a) 110.5 (b) 121

   (c) 110 (d) 100

   (E) Probability of an event is a ......

   (a) measure of chance of occurrence of event.

   (b) measure of average time for occurrence of event.

   (c) measure of numbers of times event occurs.

   (d) measure of deviation from actual chance of occurrence of event.

   (F) If $X \to B$ (n = 10, p = 0.4) then which of the following statement is true

   (a) mean = 5 (b) variance = 1

   (c) the distribution is bimodal (d) the distribution is symmetric

   (G) The normal distribution with mean μ and standard deviation σ has ......

   (a) mean = variance (b) mean > variance

   (c) mean < variance (d) mean = mode = median

(S.1)

(H) The time series is useful in ……
   (a) finding mean
   (b) finding standard deviation
   (c) comparison of the performance in past and present
   (d) finding probabilities

(I) The moving average is used to find ……
   (a) period of cycle   (b) trend in time series
   (c) predict the values in future   (d) irregular component

(J) The item is defective if ……
   (a) it is useless
   (b) it is broken
   (c) it does not confirm the specifications
   (d) too old, out dated

2. (a) Describe the theoretical basis of control charts. (5)
   (b) Construct a suitable control chart and comment whether the process is in statistical control. (5)

Aeroplane Number	1	2	3	4	5	6	7	8	9	10
Number of defects	8	10	11	8	9	8	16	7	8	5

OR

2. (a) Describe the components of time series. (5)
   (b) Estimate the trend by 3 yearly moving averages. (5)

Year	2005	2006	2007	2008	2009	2010	2011	2012
prices	16	18	20	19	21	23	28	30

3. (a) Describe the important properties of normal distribution. (5)
   (b) If the height (in cm) of individuals is normally distributed with mean 160 cm and standard deviation 10 cm. Find :
      (i) probability that an individual selected at random will have height more than 170 cm.
      (ii) the number of individuals out of 100 having height more than 170 cm.

   (The area under SNV curve between $z = 0$ and $z = 1$ is 0.3413 and that between $z = 0$ and $z = 2$ is 0.4772).

OR

3. (a) Discuss the uses and limitations of index numbers. (5)
   (b) Compute Laspreyre's, Paasche's and Fisher's index numbers for the following data :

Commodity	Princes in		Quantities in	
	Base Year ₹	Current year ₹	Base year kg	Current year kg
Wheat	20	22	12	12
Rice	40	50	5	4
Sugar	30	36	6	7
Dal	70	75	3	2

   Interpret the result. (5)

4. (a) Describe the various criteria for detecting lack of statistical control situations in control charts. (5)
   (b) Construct a P chart and comment on the state of control. (5)

Sample No.	1	2	3	4	5	6	7	8	9	10	Total
Size of sample	100	100	100	100	100	100	100	100	100	100	1000
Number of defectives	4	6	8	7	3	5	8	2	3	4	50

OR

4. (a) Distinguish between seasonal variations and cyclical variations. (3)
   (b) If the number of students get selected in an interview follows binomial distribution with n = 10, and p = 0.3. Find the :
   (i) probability that exactly 3 will be selected.
   (ii) probability that at most 3 will be selected.
   (iii) probability that none of them will be selected.
   (iv) average number of students selected. (7)

5. Draw an appropriate control chart and comment on the control of the process.

Sample No.	1	2	3	4	5	6	7	8	9	10
$\bar{X}$	23	35	31	41	29	38	46	19	15	40
R	12	19	14	21	17	23	25	16	28	15

   Given for n = 5, $A_2 = 0.58$, $D_3 = 0$, $D_4 = 2.11$. (10)

OR

5. Fit a straight line trend equation for the following time series data :

Year	1	2	3	4	5
Sales in lacks ₹	3	4	5	5	6

   Estimate the sales for year 6 and 7. (10)

Notes

www.ingramcontent.com/pod-product-compliance
Lightning Source LLC
Chambersburg PA
CBHW080343170426
43194CB00014B/2668